The Principal as Hu
Resources Leader

Increasingly, personnel administrative duties within schools have been delegated to the local school principal. This accessible book arms school leaders with the knowledge and skills required to be effective human resources leaders and shows them how to fold these additional duties seamlessly into their daily routines. This practical resource provides school administrators with guidance on personnel selection, growth and development, orientation and placement, school climate, legal processes, leadership for classified staff, and other important human resources processes.

Special Features:

- Grounded in extensive research and interviews with practicing principals
- Provides a wealth of examples, strategies, tips, and best practices for leading the human resources function at the school level
- Chapter exercises and case studies explore the skills and knowledge needed for effective human resource leadership
- Details the significance of developing a positive school climate
- Legal aspects of human resources administration are made digestible and understandable

Dr. M. Scott Norton is a former public school teacher, coordinator of curriculum, assistant superintendent, and superintendent of schools. He has served as Professor and Vice-Chair of the Department of Educational Administration at the University of Nebraska—Lincoln and as Professor and Chair of the Department of Educational Administration and Policy Studies at Arizona State University, where he is currently Professor Emeritus.

Other Eye On Education Books Available from Routledge (www.routledge.com/eyeoneducation)

The Principal as Student Advocate
A Guide for Doing What's Best for All Students
M. Scott Norton, Larry K. Kelly, and Anna R. Battle

The Principal as Instructional Leader
A Practical Handbook, Third Edition
Sally J. Zepeda

Leading Schools in an Era of Declining Resources
J. Howard Johnston and Ronald Williamson

The School Leader's Guide to Formative Assessment
Using Data to Improve Student and Teacher Achievement
Todd Stanley and Jana Alig

The School Leader's Guide to Social Media
Ronald Williamson and J. Howard Johnston

The Principalship from A to Z
Ronald Williamson and Barbara R. Blackburn

Data Analysis for Continuous School Improvement
Third Edition
Victoria Bernhardt

The Trust Factor
Strategies for School Leaders
Julie Peterson Combs, Stacey Edmonson, and Sandra Harris

What Great Principals Do Differently
18 Things That Matter Most, Second Edition
Todd Whitaker

Creating Safe Schools
A Guide for School Leaders, Teachers, and Parents
Franklin P. Schargel

The Principal as Human Resources Leader

A Guide to Exemplary Practices for Personnel Administration

M. Scott Norton

NEW YORK AND LONDON

First published 2015
by Routledge
711 Third Avenue, New York, NY 10017

and by Routledge
2 Park Square, Milton Park, Abingdon, Oxon, OX14 4RN

Routledge is an imprint of the Taylor & Francis Group, an Informa business

Library of Congress Cataloging in Publication Data
Norton, M. Scott.
The principal as human resources leader: a guide to exemplary practices for personnel administration/M. Scott Norton.
pages cm
Includes bibliographical references and index.
1. School personnel management. 2. School principals. I. Title.
LB2831.5.N67 2015
371.2′01—dc23
2014003791

ISBN: 978–1-138–02439–7 (hbk)
ISBN: 978–1-138–02440–3 (pbk)
ISBN: 978–1-315–77577–7 (ebk)

Typeset in Bembo and Helvetica Neue
by Florence Production Ltd, Stoodleigh, Devon, UK

Contents

Meet the Author

M. Scott Norton, a former public school teacher, coordinator of curriculum, assistant superintendent and superintendent of schools, served as Professor and Vice-Chair of the Department of Educational Administration and Supervision at the University of Nebraska-Lincoln, later becoming Professor and Chair of the Department of Educational Administration and Policy Studies at Arizona State University, where he is currently Professor Emeritus. His primary graduate teaching areas include classes in human resources administration, school superintendency, school principalship, educational leadership and competency-based administration.

Dr. Norton is author of college textbooks in the areas of human resources administration and the school superintendency, and has co-authored other books on the school principal as a student advocate, the school principal as a learning leader and administrative management. His latest textbook, *Competency-Based Leadership: A Guide for High Performance in the Role of School Principal*, was published by Rowman and Littlefield Education in 2013. He has published widely in national journals in such areas as teacher retention, teacher load, retention of quality school principals, organizational climate, support personnel in schools, employee assistance programs, distance education and others.

He has received several state and national awards honoring his services and contributions to the field of educational administration from such organizations as the American Association of School Administrators, the University Council for School Administrators, the Arizona School Administrators Association and the Arizona Educational Research Organization. He has also received the Arizona State University College of Education Dean's Award for excellence in service to the field, and the distinguished service award from the Arizona Education Information Service.

Dr. Norton's state and national leadership positions have included service as Executive Director of the Nebraska Association of School Administrators, a member of the Board of Directors for the Nebraska Congress of Parents and Teachers, President of the Arizona School Administrators Higher Education Division, Arizona School Administrators Board of Directors, Staff Associate of the University Council for School Administrators, Treasurer for the University Council for School Administrators, and Nebraska State Representative for the National Association of Secondary School Principals. He also has served on the Board of Editors for the American Association of School Public Relations.

Preface

This book emphasizes six major foundations for the study of the human resources function as related to the work of the school principal: (1) The Principal as Human Resources Leader, (2) Leadership for Implementing the Human Resources Processes at the Local School Level, (3) Providing for Personal and Professional Growth and Development for All School Personnel, (4) School Climate: A School Principal's Magic Wand, (5) Human Resources Administration and the Legal World of the School Principal, and (6) How the School Principal Can Actively Lead the Support Staff of the School.

Each chapter begins with a statement of the primary goal that directs the primary student learning objectives. Significant terms are defined and set in bold print.

Figures and meaningful snapshots are included to extend and/or explain certain concepts.

Each chapter is summarized and followed by chapter discussion questions that serve to provide opportunities for the reader to apply chapter concepts and to extend the chapter's concepts.

Case studies at the close of each chapter provide opportunities for the student or reader to take over the role of the school principal and to perform required human resources solutions or to implement appropriate professional personnel decisions. Case studies are such that each can be completed by an individual student or carried out as class session group activity. The references at the end of each chapter provide opportunities for extended reading by the student or practicing school principal.

The author served for many years as the director of the University Council for Educational Administration (UCEA) Program Center for Preparation Programs in Educational Administration. This position provided ongoing opportunities for research in the field of educational administration and the work of school leaders. For example, studies of the status of the school superintendent, the school principal and the human resources director were administered periodically and distributed nationally to principals and all members of UCEA. The human resources director was studied every five years; the first study was initiated in 1983 and the last in 2009. Human resources directors were asked many questions in several specific study areas, including: (1) Professional training and experience; (2) Personal and professional sociological data; (3) Work responsibilities, time commitments and work habits; (4) Problems/Challenges facing them; (5) Existing conditions; (6) Evaluation of performance; and (7) Work relationships with the district personnel office. As previously indicated, similar studies of the school principal also were administered and disseminated.

In addition, during the interim of 2010 and 2013, personal interviews were conducted with elementary, middle and secondary school principals that centered on their work as learning leaders and as leaders of the human resources function in their school. Most interviews were conducted in a face-to-face manner; others were completed by telephone. The participating principals were selected on the basis of their school's student performance rating. That is, schools that were rated by the state as being "high performance" schools were selected. These schools also were given grade-letters by the state department (A, B, C, etc.) relative to testing evidence and annual student improvement. Only schools with grades of "A" were selected.

The text places emphasis on the major responsibilities of the local school principal in the area of human resources administration by:

- Emphasizing the changing scene of the human resources function in education and its primary implications for leadership at the local school level.
- Giving attention to the changing nature of the human resources function, from a maintenance function to a strategic function that requires new skills and leadership on the part of local school leaders.
- Describing the significant role of the school principal as it relates to the "people aspects" of school administration.
- Presenting specific research, examples of best practices and case studies that focus on the skills and knowledge needed by practicing school leaders for effective practice in personnel management.
- Emphasizing the paramount importance of organizational climate in the school and its influence on personnel motivation and student academic achievement.

- Presenting the legal aspects of human resources administration that must be practiced in the work of the local school principal today. Although attention is given to best practices for implementing the HR processes in schools today, a look to the future extensions of the HR function at the local school level is projected as well.
- Providing models and examples of successful practices in human resources administration that give the reader a solid foundation for better understanding the required human resources practices of the school principal.
- Underscoring the importance of the school's support staff in relation to the human resources needs of the school.

CHAPTER

1

The Principal as Human Resources Leader

Primary chapter goal:

To understand the changing nature of the human resources function in education and the requirements of new knowledge and skills on the part of the local school principal.

The Story of Amelia

Amelia Beetison was a social studies teacher at Wymore Middle School for 22 years. She was serving as a member of the social studies curriculum committee for the Wymore School District. The coordinator of curriculum for the middle schools in Wymore, Brian Randall, was leading the committee toward the goal of updating the social studies curriculum for grades seven through nine.

During one informal visit with Dr. Randall, Amelia invited him to visit her classroom. For one reason or another, Dr. Randall did not follow up on this invitation. Toward the close of the committee's curriculum work, Amelia said to Dr. Randall, "My invitation is still open, drop by my classroom at anytime."

Dr. Randall understood that Amelia was serious about her invitation and made a courtesy call to the school principal indicating his intention to visit Amelia's classroom. Principal Lyons welcomed the visit.

Dr. Randall arrived at the school, checked in at the school's office and went directly to Amelia's classroom. He observed the teacher's social studies instruction and the involvement of the students for about one hour. As the class ended and students had left the room, Amelia met Dr. Randall at the classroom door. Amelia asked, "Well, what did you think?" The coordinator remembered his lessons on classroom supervision suggesting that the first classroom visit was simply to establish some rapport and to refrain from any serious comments about the lesson's accomplishments. He replied, "Well, I appreciated the opportunity to visit the class and perhaps I can do so again in the near future."

"That would be fine," said Amelia, "But what do you have to say about today's class session?"

Since Amelia was standing at the classroom door somewhat blocking Dr. Randall's ability to leave the room, he thought that he had to respond. He had been highly impressed with the outstanding teaching ability of Amelia and the learning environment that she had created for students in the class.

"Well," replied Dr. Randall, "If every social studies class in Wymore demonstrated the teaching competency that I observed during the last class hour, I would be out of a job."

Amelia's appreciation was expressed by the smile on her face and the evidence of tears in her eyes. To hear a sincere compliment about her long tenure of quality teaching was a reward that she greatly appreciated and most deservedly received.

Keep in Mind That Schools Are People

Talented teachers deserve as much time and attention as marginal teachers. Trophies and certificates can be appropriate rewards, but sincere verbal feedback takes little time and goes a long way. Human resources (HR) administration at the local school level encompasses more than recruiting, selecting and assigning personnel. In this chapter and in the following chapters of this book, we talk about the important basic processes of the human resources function at the local school level, but also give due emphasis to the related processes of human motivation that underscore the fact that schools are people. School climate considerations, talent management, teacher retention and other factors such as work-life balance have become important responsibilities in the work of the school principal. Always keep in mind that schools are people.

Throughout the book, we focus on the human resources function and its several related processes (see Figure 1.1). In the following section, we take a look at the school principal as a human resources leader in an ever-changing and redefined administrative role.

HR Environment →	HR Utilization →	HR Development
School Climate Process	Planning Process	Performance Evaluation Process Assessment Evaluation
Safety and Protection Process	Recruitment Process	Growth and Development Process
Work-Life Process	Selection Process	
	Orientation Process	
	Assignment Process	
	Compensation and Welfare Process	
	Stability Process Talent Management Personnel Retention	

FIGURE 1.1. The Human Resources Function and Its Primary Processes

The School Principalship: An Increasingly Redefined Role

The one certain happening in the role of school principal is that of change. Schools are social systems that improve as people grow and develop. Today the practicing school principal is expected to be competent in every administrative function, including being a learning leader, a student advocate, a community-relations expert, a student achievement promoter and, increasingly, being a human resources administrator. Yet the evidence shows that school principals themselves do not believe that their preparation programs served them satisfactorily for administering many of their stated responsibilities and the HR function is no exception.

Heretofore, the primary responsibilities for the recruiting, hiring, orientation and development of the school's staff were carried out primarily by the district's central personnel office. Today, most school principals are involved in most every process related to the HR function. For example, local school principals have become much more involved in the identification of prospective applicants for school positions and in the follow-up processes of developing position descriptions and taking a leading part in the interviewing process, especially the interviewing of final candidates for teaching positions. In addition, HR processes such as performance appraisals have had many changes that require pre-conferences, advanced notices for teacher observations, required instruments for assessment, post-conferences and the development of follow-up plans for personal improvement. Empirical evidence indicates that the development of position analyses for professional personnel is limited at best. But let us give thought to how this activity could serve you and your personnel. A position analysis precedes the development of a specific position description.

Analyzing and Describing Every Position

Why analyze and describe every position? Two primary reasons center on legal concerns. First, the Equal Opportunity Act no longer leaves a choice in the matter. An analysis is needed to defend your personnel practices. In personnel litigation cases, the employee's position description becomes the center of attention. In addition, change that is constantly occurring in your school alters the responsibilities of jobs for both the professional and support staffs.

A position analysis commonly requires the following information:

1. The position itself (duties, tools, load, supervision);
2. Qualifications (knowledge, skills, certifications, experience, physical requirements);
3. Schedule (time requirements, tasks that influence the role, community requirements, development requirements);
4. Effects of the position on the employee (stress, health, relationships, turnover, physical factors such as sitting, standing, walking);
5. Relationship to the organization (supervision, reporting responsibilities, coordination, communication activities, accountabilities);
6. Relationships to the school-community (support services, responsibilities, communication, involvement, contacts).

It is not uncommon to find that the position description of a school principal includes only a general statement to the effect that the school principal is responsible for the professional and support personnel within the school. The following excerpt from the high school principal's position description of the Council Rock School District of Bucks County, Pennsylvania sets forth a more definitive personnel administration responsibility.

> POSITION SUMMARY
>
> The principal is the educational leader of the school, responsible for planning, developing, coordinating, directing and evaluating the school's educational program and environment. Responsibilities include inter-

> viewing, hiring, and training employees; planning, assigning . . . appraising performance; rewarding and disciplining employees, addressing complaints and resolving problems.

In subsection 3 of the Council Rock School District position description for high school principals, essential functions and responsibilities include the following personnel administration entries: (i) Assisting the central office in the recruitment, interviewing, and selection of new teachers and other staff members; (ii) Organizing, administering and utilizing staff effectively; (iii) Inducting and orienting professional and support staff; and (iv) Evaluating, rating, and recommending the dismissal of staff.

Don't Try to Wing It: Continuous Self-Development Looms Important

Research evidence supports the fact that the large majority of school principals are not prepared to carry out effectively the activities of the HR function. When asked, school principals commonly state that they are learning how to administer the school's personnel processes on the job, or that they tend to confer with colleagues about personnel procedures. According to a report of one research organization (Hess & Kelly, 2005), only 36 percent of school principals believed that their attention to marginal teachers was leading to appropriate tenure denials. On-the-job learning most often falls short of implementing the best personnel practices. As noted by Deadrick and Stone (2009), researchers and practitioners may need to step back and review past discoveries, studies and research to ensure that the field of human research development continues to advance with development of theory, contributory research, and input for practice. Just becoming a school principal certainly does not automatically make the individual competent as an effective candidate interviewer or judge of quality hires.

More sophisticated methods for such HR processes as the hiring of teachers, professional development, performance evaluation, results accountability and school climate improvement are being required of practicing school principals. "Some of the biggest changes have occurred in recruiting, compensation and training" (Greengard, 2012, p. 5). In an article by Hess and Kelly (2005), the authors reported findings on school principals' work preparation as revealed in their courses of study. The principal-preparation programs examined devoted barely 3 percent of total instructional weeks in core courses to the central management responsibilities of hiring, identifying, and rewarding good employees, or identifying and removing ineffective ones.

Movement Toward Site-Based Management and Its Implications for New Leadership

The realization that many of the administrative processes were moving from the school district's central offices to the local schools is not a yesterday's happening. Richard Smith (1998), among other HR authorities, discussed this phenomenon in his book, *Human Resources Administration: A School-Based Perspective*, more than a decade ago. As noted by Smith (1998):

> One of the major changes in education is the movement toward school-based leadership. Many of the management functions which were previously centralized for control and standardization are now being decentralized . . . where they become the responsibility of the school principal. . . . The principal's ability to provide effective leadership to the human resources function of the school will, in large measure, determine the effectiveness of the school and the teachers.
>
> (p. 5)

New Takes on HR Processes Can Lead to Improved Results

Schmidt and Hunter (1998) recommend a variety of methods for judging the interviews: intelligence tests, integrity tests, assessment-center results, biographical data and others. The hiring authority might utilize a test of general intelligence and a test of integrity to calculate a valid statistic for predicting the future job performance of a particular candidate. But is all this time and effort worth the trouble that it takes to prepare and implement? It most certainly is, according to Schmidt and Hunter (1998), who used a general intelligence test and combined it with several other tests such as an integrity test, work-sample tests, and assessment-center results. They found that the general intelligence test coupled with the integrity test gave the highest validity result of 0.65. The lowest validity combination came with the general intelligence test and assessment results, the validity statistic of which was 0.53. Such results serve to provide additional hard data for improving hiring decisions.

The point here is that the opportunity to increase one's knowledge and skill for hiring decisions is available. Personal judgments about a candidate's qualities often are based on subjective evidence that is not directly related to the candidate's true qualifications. Both personal interview judgments and the candidate's personal references are often misleading and unrelated to the knowledge and skills necessary for success on the job. HR processes such as recruitment, selection, assignment and others, to be effective, must be carefully planned; research in these areas will prove to be of much value to you as well.

It should be clear to all concerned that just being appointed to the responsible position of school principal does not guarantee that he or she has the required knowledge and skills for conducting effective hiring interviews or making final hiring decisions. Skill and knowledge in these areas can be attained, and Chapter 2 of this text discusses the selection process in detail.

Let's Check Your Accountability Status

Assume that a school's teacher retention rate over the last three years was 55 percent. That is, 55 percent of the teachers hired three years ago still remain on the faculty. Which of the following entries would be most productive for assessing the effectiveness of retention procedures utilized by the school? Each entry most likely would produce some useful information, but identify the entries that would most likely provide important hard data related to retention program results.

1. Data on the percentage of teachers that attended the school's 12-hour in-service program on assessment techniques relative to student achievement.
2. The identification of the specific activities implemented by the school principal to retain teachers in the school.
3. The opportunities provided for professional growth for the school's teachers during the three-year time period.
4. The climate-improvement programs/procedures that were implemented during the three-year time period.
5. Assessment data providing the results of the induction program for teachers who entered the school in one of the three years, in terms of teacher tenure, job-satisfaction measures and improvements in student achievement.
6. An analysis of the results of the planned balanced work-life provisions/activities for faculty/support personnel, in terms of retention, job satisfaction and student achievement improvement.
7. Collected evidence that faculty members know and understand the organizational mission of the school, and specifically, evidence such as performance-evaluation results and examinations of lesson plans that reveal that instruction in the classrooms of the school is centered on the mission's goals and objectives.

8. An analysis of the system in place to provide an opportunity for personnel to challenge the way things are done in the school; being able to speak up about the status quo without fear of retribution. What hard data were gathered to ascertain the system's effectiveness, and what did the analysis reveal?
9. Evidence collected to determine that teacher placements were in subject-matter area(s) of major preparation and interests, and that extracurricular assignments were made according to the teacher's expressed interests.
10. The implementation of a variety of specific measurements of the school's climate from the perspective of teachers, parents and students, and an analysis of the data resulting from the assessments.

Answers: Questions 1 through 4 above are most likely to collect soft data that provide little information about improvement results. Each of the other entries, 5 through 10, has the potential of providing valuable information about the effectiveness and value of the respective activities. For example, entries 5, 6, 7, 8, 9 and 10, if implemented, would provide significant evidence related to the effectiveness of the hiring, induction and climate processes. If you answered 8 to 10 of the entries correctly, your thinking on the accountability scale is very good. A score of 5 to 7 is good, but there is room for improvement. A score of 0 to 4, however, indicates that accountability improvement is needed. This chapter and the following chapters will provide additional guidance that will lead to improvement in the accountability arena.

Principals and selection teams must be held accountable for hiring results. Filling positions alone is no longer enough. To what extent have hires evidenced effectiveness in contributing to the mission, goals and objectives of the school's program? Have faculty and support personnel shown a commitment to achieving the primary school goals? Hard data that reveal the retention or early departure of teachers and support staff are required. What activities have been effective in keeping quality personnel on the job? Have the administrative personnel been effective in the selection process? Such factors as student achievement, tenure history, and teacher absenteeism are indicators of effective or ineffective hires.

Accountability and the Costs of Teacher Absenteeism

Teacher absenteeism is an ongoing problem that practicing school principals must face. Its impact on student achievement, budget expenditures, program effectiveness and teacher professionalism are among the various educational concerns. The school principal's responsibilities must include attention to the results of the absenteeism phenomenon. Research has not provided a solution to the issue of loss of student achievement due to a teacher's absence, but approximate monetary calculations do show serious budgetary results. For example, consider the case of a school district with 420 teachers who work 40 hours per week on the average for 40 weeks. Cacio (2003) reports that absenteeism accounts for 1.75 percent of the scheduled work hours. Assume that teachers receive an average hourly salary of $70.

> 40 hr × 40 weeks = 1,600 hr
>
> 2 weeks vacation or 40 × 2 = 80 hr
>
> 5 paid holidays or 5 × 8 = 40 hr
>
> 1,600 hr – (80 hr + 40 hr) = 1,480 hr
>
> 1,480 × 420 teachers = 621,600 total scheduled hrs
>
> 621,600 × 0.0175 = 10,878 hours lost per year
>
> 10,878 × $70 = $761,460 cost per year, not counting expenses for substitute teachers and other related expenses.

> Accountability, as it relates to the work of the HR function, is revealed in the extent to which it establishes procedures and initiatives to deal with changes in the workplace, to attend appropriately with diversity, and to implement programs that provide evidence of their contributions to the goals of the school system.
>
> (Norton, 2008, p. 21)

Accountability, like all other effective program activities, requires attention to meaningful planning, programmed implementation and ongoing evaluation. Human resources accountability is the responsibility of all members of the school's professional and support staff. Accountability is revealed in a variety of ways related to the human resources processes. For example, the implementation of effective assessments of a school's climate is one measure of accountability. That is, accountability is revealed in the HR process of orientation when the process takes place in a healthy school environment. As will be discussed in detail in Chapter 4, a positive school climate fosters student academic achievement as well as increased teacher retention. Empirical evidence suggests that beginning teachers do not understand the importance of their role in the development of a positive school climate. Teacher-preparation programs have tended to leave a serious gap between the understanding of school-climate factors and their responsibilities in the area of teaching and learning. The HR process of staff development looms important in closing this information gap. Special in-service programs in school climate are essential for school improvement efforts.

A model for assessing accountability effectiveness is outlined in the following section. It provides guidelines for you and your school staff for implementing school program activities, and presents challenging opportunities for changes that meet the unique needs of the school.

A Model for Guiding Accountability Practices

- **Guideline 1**—Identifying the human resources process, problem or target areas to be assessed. If the hiring process is to be assessed, for example, select the specific activities within the process to be targeted, such as the training of interviewers, selection interview techniques, or assessment of selection results.
- **Guideline 2**—Selection of members of the assessment team. It is especially important that team members have human resources experience or have participated in professional development sessions that prepare them for this responsibility. Experience in the target area to be assessed also is important.
- **Guideline 3**—Identify the sources of support in relation to the target areas being addressed. What information will be needed to conduct the assessment, and how will it be collected?
- **Guideline 4**—How will the collected information/data be analyzed and reported? This includes the statistical treatments to be applied, data analysis and reporting strategies.
- **Guideline 5**—Complete a first draft of assessment results. Double-check the report and report statistics for accuracy. Have significant others review the preliminary assessment report.
- **Guideline 6**—Complete the final assessment report with appropriate recommendations. Report must be objective and truthfully reported. Both positive and negative data must be reported honestly.
- **Guideline 7**—Identify the appropriate follow-up improvement teams. What is the most appropriate unit(s) to serve as the improvement team?
- **Guideline 8**—An appraisal of the assessment procedures is recommended. It serves as the final step in the accountability assessment model.

Completing the implementation of the foregoing accountability plan will serve the school's purposes in several strategic ways. The parents, school board, state board of education and various legislative bodies are demanding program accountability on the part of education. Taking a proactive position by completing an accountability assessment and reporting it to the general public will tend to reduce the wave of criticism that can be expected without such a well-planned assessment. The topic of accountability is discussed additionally in the remaining chapters of this book.

New Challenges for Providing a Balanced Work-Life for School Personnel

Teachers teach because they just love kids, not for money, right? Yes, some teachers indeed are student advocates and consider the needs and interests of learners as their first priority. However, it is quite clear today that having a balanced work-life is a requirement of today's teachers. Life outside the classroom looms important to teachers today. As noted by Heathfield (2013), "managing millennials is a skill managers need to develop. The millennial quest for work-life balance and for having a life outside of work is legend." Millennials are individuals born in the years 1981 to 2000. This age group includes individuals that will be entering or have already entered the teaching profession.

A recent article by Zeitler (2013) listed the top seven trends in human resources. Trend number three on the list was "Work-life balance is more important than status." Concordia University Online (2013) reported Claudia Graziano's research on the importance of a balanced work-life for teachers in the statement that

> 45 percent of teachers have quit the profession after a mere five years, with stress-related burnout playing a major role in this attrition. A teacher who fails to strike a balance between work and private life risks becoming disillusioned, mentally overwhelmed or emotionally unstable.

The work-life bottom line is that an organization that does not recognize the needs of employees for having a life outside of work will lose them to an organization that will.

Work-life provisions in organizations include such provisions as work schedules, childcare provisions, eldercare assistance, health benefits, part-time

Preparing and Delivering Classroom Instruction	Pursuing Personal Wellness
Student Relations	Scheduling Recreational Activities
Parental Relations	Flexible Work Assignments
Extracurricular Assignments	Time Off
Reports and Paperwork	Family Responsibilities
Committee Assignments	Eldercare Responsibilities
Faculty Meetings	Personal Leave Provisions
Professional Association Work	Assignments Based on Personal Strengths and Interests
	Purposeful Management of Time
WORK	LIFE

FIGURE 1.2. Selected Work-Life Balance Factors

flexibility work, leave provisions, and balanced work-life policies and regulations (see Figure 1.2). Studies commonly agree that workplaces with greater flexibility are more likely to have employees who are more engaged, in better health, more satisfied with their jobs, and more likely to remain on the job (Galinsky, 2010).

Some aspects of flexibility might not work well in schools. For example, working at home certainly does not fit the common school classroom setting. Nevertheless, remote work arrangements increasingly are transforming the workplaces in organizations nationally. Schools can utilize such flexibility in the forms of part-time teaching schedules, flexibility in leave policies related to illness, childcare, caregiving, and approved volunteer work. One seldom hears the provision of sabbatical leaves in education for teachers or school administrators. It appears to work successfully at institutions of higher education, so why not at K–12 levels? Such extended time off could benefit both the employee and the school district. The teacher might focus on a project that advances his or her career, while the school district gains by the new knowledge and vigor gained by the employee from the extended experience. A sabbatical leave policy could be administered in connection with the school district's leave policies. But such a flexible arrangement couldn't work in K–12 schools, or could it? However, if a certain kind of flexibility does not work in the school, the principal can implement other kinds of work-life balances that do meet employee needs.

In several instances, practicing principals described their implementation of assignment flexibility at a time when a talented elementary teacher was about to resign due to the need to provide care for a family member. In one case, the teacher could work for one half-day only. The principal worked diligently to find another highly qualified teacher to assume the classroom responsibilities for the other one half-day. Did this arrangement work? It did in each of the several cases that were reported.

The key to a successful result in these arrangements, of course, is finding a qualified second teacher to assume the one-half day teaching assignment. In the case described above, that teacher was a retired teacher that readily accepted the position.

How can the principal determine such needs of the faculty and support staff? You ask them! In this way, the school principal can get a sense of what really matters to the school personnel.

Providing for a Balanced Work-Life for Teachers: What Teachers Say

Interviews were conducted with a sample of classroom teachers. The interviews focused on the question of what they believed to be important for them in realizing a balanced work-life. Most responses came in the form of what each teacher identified as what worked for them. A few examples of teachers' partial responses were as follows:

Teacher 1—"There is always something that we must do. I do my best to place the needs and interests of my students and family first. I then prioritize the work/responsibility in terms of what I believe is first priority (must be done now), second priority (must be done but it can wait) and third or no priority (wait and see if time permits). This procedure gives me a positive feeling that I am doing the best for my students and my family members. You can't put family and friends at the bottom of your 'to do' list. In keeping family and friends among my priorities, I think that I am also doing what is best for me."

Teacher 2—"I have found that facing a problem matter directly and doing my best to solve it in the end is best for me. Rather than to wait and worry, I move to assess and address the problem. I am always surprised by the number of problems that are resolved much easier than I expected them to be. Worrying about the matter never helped much. It only left me with a feeling of frustration and depression. Resolution most often results with a feeling of being refreshed and renewed."

Teacher 3—"I keep a weekly notebook that notes the time spent on teaching, meetings, phone calls, emails and family matters and personal interests and needs. This is not a diary or detailed record of time and events, but a short note to remind me of the matter at hand and the time it took. In some cases I note what went well and what did not go as well in the situation. At the end of the week, I take one hour to be myself and go over the notes. What went especially well and why? What did not go so well and why not? This hour of self-reflection has done more for me regarding my work-life balance and personal relationships than any other activity of personal growth that I have attempted."

Teacher 4—"Good things happen when the school principal understands the teacher's needs for a balanced work-life. A large part of it comes with the principal's knowing his or her staff, having a knowledge of teacher load research and acknowledging the efforts of school personnel in regard to the school's mission."

Teacher 5—"When I joined the staff of my present school, the first thing that the principal asked me was about my strengths and professional interests. I was somewhat surprised that she used my responses both in my instructional assignments but in my extra-curricular assignments as well. She even asked me to be the sponsor of an after-school activity in my interest area of dance. When the activity was announced, there was standing room only in the classroom for the initial after school meeting of interested students. I was able to relate my outside school interests in dance to my extra-curricular sponsorship of dance at school. I think that work-life balance is related to work-life interests."

Teacher 6—"Each time that I observe or hear about a faculty or support staff member doing something that deserves a special note of thanks, I send them a memo that has a picture of a black crow on the front and a saying, 'Something to crow about' . . . and then I list my name. I write a short piece of thanks and note about what I think the teacher's or support staff member's activity contributed to our school's mission. This response to positive behavior takes no more than a few minutes yet seems to be remembered by the school member for a long time. On one occasion I was called to the front of the meeting room to receive a pin from our local parent teacher organization for my service to the organization. One member of our school faculty called out, 'Now that's something to crow about!' Everyone laughed; the phrase 'something to crow about' apparently had caught on."

Human Resources Administration and Its Influence on Student Achievement

It is clear that the climate of the school has a direct influence on the status of student achievement (Hoy & Appleberry, 1970; Deibert & Hoy, 1977; Lunenburg, 1983; Hopkins & Crain, 1985; Paredes & Frazer, 1992; Winter & Sweeney, 1994). For example, Winter and Sweeney (1994) note that climate not only affects student achievement but it also is revealed in the attitudes, beliefs and values held by the people in the school. Research also has made it clear that the school principal serves as the key individual for influencing the health of the school climate.

> One guidepost offered by research suggests that principals influence teaching and learning by creating a safe and supportive school climate . . . because principals tend to have *direct* influence on school conditions . . . such as school climate . . . and creating conditions within a school for better teaching and learning to occur.
>
> (Clifford et al., 2012, p. 2)

The HR processes responsibilities that influence student achievement are discussed specifically later in Chapter 2. As previously noted, the topic of school climate is the primary consideration discussed in Chapter 4. Each of these chapters extends the relationship of the human resources function and the need for leadership in this area by the school principal.

Talent Management: The Challenges Facing School Leaders

Talent management has become an essential HR responsibility of the practicing school principal. It focuses on the school leader's efforts to identify the personal strengths and interests of each employee and to utilize these strengths in assigning work responsibilities in the plan to achieve the school's stated goals and objectives. Talent management places emphasis on employee engagement, employee turnover and talent acquisition. Attention also is given to strengthening any identified weaknesses of the employee, but the primary focus is placed on the employee's strengths as opposed to his or her weaknesses. As Clifton and Nelson (1992) have emphasized, people soar with their strengths.

When school administrators are asked what is being done to retain talented faculty members, the common answer is "not much." This is a significant concern, since most everyone would agree that schools, like any other successful organization, need talented personnel to meet stated goals and objectives. Yet the evidence shows on a continuous basis that 50 percent of the teachers entering the teaching profession will leave the profession by the end of five years.

> Talent management is the science of using strategic HR to improve business value and to make it possible for companies and organizations

> to reach their goals. Everything done to recruit, retain, develop and reward and make people perform forms a part of talent management. (Wikipedia, 2013)

Social media for recruiting and wellness initiatives are among the recent trends in HR management. The need is not only to attract talented personnel, but time and effort must be devoted to orienting, developing and training talent; each is an important HR process.

What School Principals Must Do to Achieve Talent Management Objectives

You can take specific steps to help retain talent within your school. The following steps are ones that serve that purpose.

- Successful results demand cooperative decision-making relative to the purposes of the work itself and mutual agreement as to the assessments to be utilized in measuring the success. Agreement between the school principal and the teacher concerning the goals and objectives of class instruction gives the teacher a feeling of freedom to utilize personal strengths in relation to teaching methods. The supervisor benefits as well by knowing that the goals and objectives utilized to direct the instruction tie closely to the school's mission and its related goals and objectives. It also sets the foundation for determining the assessment of student achievement, and thus contributes immeasurably to the factor of accountability.
- Cooperative decision-making serves as a basis for determining the plan for the teacher's self-directed professional development. In the end, the best professional development is self-development. It would appear impossible to find a teacher that does not want to become a better teacher, and experience has shown that professional teachers are willing to accept personal responsibility for the results of their teaching when they have had an opportunity to implement their autonomy in teaching. The topic of professional growth and development is discussed in depth in Chapter 3.
- Talent management includes the school principal's role as a coach. **Coaching**, however, goes beyond the work in the school and the teacher's classroom. "Coaches serve to answer the question, 'Where do you want to go?' Through the use of key listening techniques, coaches help guide the individual as he/she focuses on desired career directions" (Norton, 2008,

p. 203). The principal as a coach is a teacher's advocate that broadens the teacher's horizons while improving his/her present educational knowledge and skills.

- Talent management increasingly is a competitive process. Businesses and industries are faced with a continuous challenge to attract and retain talented employees. Schools are no exception. In education, however, monetary salaries for teachers and support staff seldom differ significantly from school district to school district. The competitive challenge for the school and school district is revealed in their ability to be more competent in recruiting, hiring, assigning and developing talent.
- Providing positive feedback and letting quality personnel know how well they are doing and how much their work is serving the purposes of the school's mission is essential.

Tips On Best Practices and Experimental Efforts to Attract and Retain Talent

It isn't that school HR administrators have not always tried to attract and hire the highest qualified personnel for positions in the school. But now the demands being made on schools to improve student achievement and to demonstrate accountability for budgetary expenditures, coupled with the need to compete in the highly competitive race for recruiting and retaining quality personnel, have made it clear to school leaders that they must take talent management much more seriously if such demands are to be met.

The following section identifies selected practices that are being implemented in school districts nationally and/or have been recommended by authorities or various educational agencies. Some initiated practices are not particularly new, but are done with needed emphasis and priority. Others that challenge long-time policies and practices are more controversial. For example, to encourage new talent to join or remain in the school, schools have curtailed seniority privileges and ended bumping practices. Tenure policies have been challenged and changed in some school districts.

It could be that successful best practices in talent management for one school do not work in another school. Nevertheless, successful practices need to be shared with other schools for their consideration. The following "best practices" are ones that have been either recommended by school leaders or set forth by educational agencies and business organizations as desirable considerations for improving talent management practices.

Development Dimensions International (Wellins et al., 2009) recommended nine best practices for effective HR management. For purposes of illustration, some of the nine best practices are summarized below.

Best Practice: How to place the right people in the right jobs.
Hiring for the right skills is more efficient than developing for those skills later. As an example, assessing such skills as decision-making, personal skills or judgment is likely to be less expensive at the time of selection than trying to develop them on the job. The importance of placing the individual in the area of his or her strengths and personal interests is essential for allowing the person to soar with their strengths. In doing so, motivation is likely to increase; poor job fit assures poor performance.

Best Practice: Talent management is more about the "hows" than the "whats."
The rationale here is that the "hows" of administering a talented staff give more promise for sound execution and positive results. For example, implementing the accountability procedures set forth previously in this chapter serve to provide position clarity and a sense of autonomy for implementation in the mind of the worker. Knowing the end expectations of a role facilitates the release of the individual's knowledge and skills to accomplish the task with the talent he or she possesses.

Best Practice: Redesigning policies and practices to support flexibility and performance relative to teacher contracts.
Giving school principals more control over hiring, curtailing seniority privileges, ending bumping practices, requiring RIF (reduction in force) teachers to reapply for positions instead of being placed in them and revising certification rules to encourage expansion of the pool of teacher applicants (e.g., business, industrial, science and individuals from other occupations) can be effective as a talent management strategy. Contemporary tenure laws tend to guarantee RIF teachers seniority in position replacements. However, the procedure of rehiring a marginal teacher when a high quality candidate is available militates against talent management efforts. Although controversial, we take the position that performance quality is a priority over the question of lifetime tenure.

Best Practice: How to establish working relations with colleges and universities.
Ongoing working relationships with colleges and universities hold many opportunities for realizing talent management purposes. Arrangements with

higher education institutions that include tuition reimbursements and summer fellows programs in exchange for internship roles in local schools are examples that foster the identification of talented educational personnel. The cooperative initiation of "grow your own" initiatives to train potential teachers and school administrators are other examples of cooperative talent management programs.

Although early hiring opportunities have potential problems related to adequate projections of school enrollments and actual personnel needs, giving the principal the ability to initiate earlier hiring in the winter and early spring rather than the late summer can open the door to recruiting talented persons before they are lost to other employment.

Best Practice: A planned talent management procedure is essential.
An effective talent management plan sets forth the primary goals and objectives, procedures for implementation, human and material resources required and specific measures for assessing the plan's results. Emphasis should be placed on closing the talent gap, and the plan should be related closely to the mission statement of goals and objectives for the school. Effective planning is of paramount importance. A strategic plan is one in which the goals and objectives tie closely to the overall goals and objectives of the school's mission statement. According to Wellins et al. (2009), only when the organization's talent plan ties closely to the organization's main business and needs will it be possible for talent management to be both effective and sustainable.

Strange as it may seem, evidence suggests that few schools have developed and implemented a formal talent action plan. Such a need likely has been informally discussed and considered to be essential, but steps that actually result in the development and implementation of such a plan often are not initiated. Education is not alone in this respect. One report indicated that only 5 percent of organizations say they have a clear and defined talent management plan in place and operating (Wikipedia, 2013).

Best Practice: Using available teacher talent for administering the school program.
Specific evidence is not available to determine what percentage of practicing teachers have aspirations for becoming a school administrator. We do know that the large majority of school assistant principals and principals are appointed from teaching positions. Within the talent of a teaching staff are teachers with work in business administration, journalism, communication, special education, technology, industrial arts, health and safety, physical education and safety, and other specialties. Capitalizing on this talent to take some responsibility for administrative activities within the school serves several primary purposes.

First, personnel that can help the school principal do inventories and compile information relative to the school's instructional needs, or help to prepare the school budget not only reduce the principal's workload, but the performance of such duties give the individuals on-site experience in a particular administrative area. In addition, using talented staff personnel to complete attractive communication brochures and written communications lends to the extension of administrative skills for these persons and puts the talents of staff personnel to work for improved communication with the school's clients.

It is not the intent here to place an additional workload on the regular staff of the school; some reduced instructional time is in order. Released time can be compensated in a variety of ways. Some programs have given graduate internship credit to teachers who are working on advanced degrees. In other instances, part-time faculty personnel have been hired to teach while the regular teacher is serving the school in another way. In either case, it results in a win-win situation.

Best Practice: Like the unchallenged student, the unchallenged teacher loses interest.

One school principal tells the story of one of his most effective teachers related to her apparent lack of interest and motivation. Mary Dearell had been teaching advanced mathematics for eleven years and had been considered a high performer. She had earned a Master's degree three years after joining the school's faculty. But over the years, she seemed to have lost interest and motivation.

The school district had expressed the need to examine the district's mathematics and science curriculum. A representative committee was selected to develop a coordinated math and science curriculum for grades 7 through 12. Curriculum guides were to be developed for each grade level. An advanced program was recommended in math that would extend the regular course work for talented students. One new addition was that of a course in calculus, and another course in vector quantities was to be developed. No member of the teachers' group had previous work in the area of vectors, and Mary was no exception.

Unknown to Mary, her principal had learned of the need for someone to take the lead in developing the course on vectors. He called the district coordinator of curriculum and suggested that she ask Mary to take the lead on the vectors curriculum guide. When Mary was asked by the curriculum director if she might be willing to work on the vector course, she said, "Sorry, but I know little or nothing about vectors."

With a little arm twisting, Mary agreed to do what she could with the project. She did her homework, counseled with her math advisor at the university and gained what other information she could from the math and science literature in the university library.

Mary completed an impressive course curriculum guide for the potential course and also completed a teacher's instruction booklet to accompany the curriculum guide. She presented the work at a meeting of the curriculum committee. The committee members' reception of Mary's work was most positive.

Mary's principal asked her if she would take the lead in offering the first course on vector quantities during the first semester of the following year. Mary readily agreed to do so. During the remainder of the school year, Mary authored an enrichment book on the topic of vector quantities for high school students. The book was published by a New York company. Additionally, the book was translated into the Spanish, German, Japanese and Italian languages. The final result was evidenced by a new math book for use by students nationally, professional growth for Mary, and a renewed talented teacher.

Retention incentives can be viewed as power rewards. Creating a climate of appreciation by helping employees to understand their importance in the system is one example of a power reward. Other such incentives are exemplified by adding a variety and interest to your faculty's work assignments, increasing employee authority and responsibility and encouraging continuous learning within the school's employees.

Retention incentives serve to develop a sense of commitment to the school on the part of the faculty and support personnel. Job satisfaction and opportunities for personal growth add to one's job commitment, as does the recognition of the need for a balanced work-life and an opportunity to know and understand the direction of the school in regard to its primary goals and objectives.

What Does It Mean for You to Possess Certain Competencies for HR Effectiveness?

An individual is appointed to lead a school as the school principal and he or she suddenly becomes the "expert" for human resources services facing the school. Unless the individual has had special preparation in human resources administration, or perhaps prior experience in the HR function as an assistant principal or in another department, he or she most likely is no better prepared to do the HR work than any other staff member. Yet significant HR decisions

Tasks	Competencies	Indicators
1.0 To determine staffing needs.	1.1 Ability to research and recommend staffing alternatives.	1.1.1 Reviews research regarding patterns and allocations.
	1.2 Ability to collect and evaluate data gathered on staffing needs.	1.2.1 Allocates staff positions based on enrollment projections.
	1.3 Ability to develop useful job descriptions.	1.3.1 Recognizes and classifies position qualifications and required position competencies.
2.0 To develop a recruitment pool.	2.1 Ability to determine the best sources of qualified candidates.	2.1.1 Develops and maintains a professional relationship with sources of full-time/part-time candidates.
		2.1.2 Uses available technology, the school faculty and other school resources to gather recommendations for potential candidates.
		2.1.3 Establishes working relationships with college/university placement offices for qualified applicants.
	2.2 Ability to implement a program of re-recruitment to retain key personnel.	2.2.1 Establishes procedures for conferring with school personnel regarding job satisfaction and their personal interests in job assignments.
	2.3 Ability to understand and comply with state regulations and the school board's formal personnel recruitment policy.	2.3.1 Reviews and follows the school board's personnel recruitment policy as related to such factors as staff balance, background checks and use of qualified personnel in the recruitment process.

FIGURE 1.3. Tasks, Competencies and Indicators of Competency Related to Staffing for Educational Services

Source: Based on *Competency-Based Preparation of Educational Administrators: Tasks, Competencies and Indicators of Competencies*, 1987, M. Scott Norton (Editor), College of Education, Arizona State University, Tempe, Arizona.

often are made as though the person were adequately prepared for the HR responsibilities.

"The term 'talent management' is usually associated with competency-based management. Talent management decisions are often driven by a set of organized core competencies as well as position-specific competencies" (Wikipedia, 2003). It is essential that the school principal understands the primary HR tasks to be addressed, is aware of the related competencies that must be learned to meet the tasks effectively and knows the indicators of the competencies that demonstrate one's knowledge and skill in a particular competency area.

A **task** is a specific responsibility, obligation or requirement associated with a professional position or function (e.g., the HR function). **Competency** refers to the ability to accomplish a task at a satisfactory level of performance. **Indicators of competency** are products or behaviors that illustrate one's capacity to perform competently. Indicators represent performance specifications (Webb & Norton, 2009). It looms important for the school principal to know and understand the tasks, competencies and indicators of competency related to the HR function in the school. It is beyond the scope of this chapter to detail the many primary tasks required of the principal for administering the HR function, but for purposes of illustration, Figure 1.3 illustrates the competency concept for one major HR task required in the school principal's role.

Summary

Schools will progress as their leaders are able to recruit, hire, orient, develop and retain quality personnel. The school principal's important leadership role has increasingly extended in the human resources function. Many of the personnel activities previously administered by the director of personnel in the school district's central office have been delegated to the principal at the local school level. However, evidence has shown that individuals who are appointed to the principalship are marginally prepared to assume the challenging personnel responsibilities required of them. Preparation programs have not emphasized the knowledge and skills related to effective personnel practices.

The nature and attitudes of personnel entering the teaching profession also have changed. The former purpose of "living to work" has changed more toward the attitude of "working to live." Work-life balance now looms important. Business and industry have learned that providing a balanced work-life is an absolute necessity for attracting and retaining talented personnel; the education profession is no exception.

Accountability for end results is being demanded on the part of educators in all endeavors. Evidence for quality results in the areas of student achievement has led to increased attention to the human resources processes of hiring, assigning, evaluating and developing school personnel. Hard data showing evidence of positive results are required. Return on investment is an important consideration. The value of program inputs is being assessed in terms of positive outcomes. Student achievement results loom important in decisions relative to the school's program provisions, teachers' performances and principals' leadership.

The recruitment and hiring of talented personnel are receiving inspired attention. Competition for talent is prevalent in education. Re-recruitment of present talent is part of the proactive efforts to increase teacher retention, a problem that has been an ongoing one for schools. Talent management has become an added process of the human resources component of the human resources function.

Competency-based leadership focuses on the primary skills, competencies and indicators of competency required of the effective HR principal. The job description of the school principal and his or her performance evaluations must include the extent to which the school principal must meet these requirements.

Discussion Questions

1. A school principal has recommended that a new gifted-student program be initiated in her school. The primary focus of the new program would center on creative writing. Along with the regular teacher, other creative writers in the community would be identified and asked to serve as part-time resource experts. Give some thought to the principal's proposal on this project. What specific program information relative to accountability would be important for the principal to consider? That is, what hard data relative to program results would serve the principal well in an attempt to gain approval to implement the new program?
2. The chapter content addresses the topic of the preparation of school principals relative to their responsibilities for administering the HR function at the local school level. Analyze the extent to which you believe school principals in America are meeting the challenges facing them in the area of HR administration. In your opinion, what positive or negative

activities can you identify relative to the current status of HR administration at the local school level?

3. **Class Exercise.** Divide the class members into several groups. Ask each group to identify what it believes to be needed provisions to improve the balance of work-life for teaching personnel. Have each group report on its recommendations, and then have the entire class membership gain consensus on the top three most important provisions.

CASE STUDIES

Case 1.1. It's Time to Get Tough on Student Retention—Or Is It?

MEMO
To: All Members of the Staff
From: Dylan Wilson, Principal
Re: Grade Retention

At our next faculty meeting on Friday, the agenda will focus primarily on the matter of pupil grading and social promotion practices. The assistant superintendent of instruction, Dr. Tyler Scott, has informed me that our school ranks eighth lowest of the ten elementary schools in the Wymore School District relative to student achievement in reading, mathematics and science.

In spite of our recent efforts to improve the academic achievement of our pupils by increasing homework assignments, offering after-school tutoring sessions, cutting the afternoon recess period and asking parents to set aside time for added study time for their children at home, we find ourselves being viewed as an underperforming school. Student absenteeism is a problem as well.

After receiving this news from Dr. Scott, I sat back and gave thought to this embarrassing problem. It seems to me that our grading system needs a serious review. Too many pupils are being promoted in grades. It's time to get tough on student retention! We need to improve student achievement.

Please be prepared to bring your recommendations for resolving this problem to our meeting on Friday. How best can we toughen our grading system? What steps can we take to improve student achievement? Higher standards need to be set.

Question:

Give some serious thought to Principal Wilson's memo. What specific responses will you make to his recommendations and questions posed? Think about the administrative actions that you would take in relation to the matter at hand. Set forth these actions briefly in writing.

Case 1.2 Certainly Do Not Want to Lose Her!

Elaine Ora has been a teacher of home economics at Wymore High School for 18 years. Her daily teaching load consists of four classes of home economics and one class of accounting. Her performance evaluations over these many years have been excellent in all categories. Elaine's leadership qualities were recognized by the fact that her colleagues had nominated her for chair of the home economics department at the school, selected her to serve on several school and district-wide committees over her years of service, and had selected her twice as teacher of the year during her tenure.

However, during the last two years of service, Elaine's absentee record had increased considerably. Due to the poor health of her mother, she had to use the full allocation of ten days of absence per year. In addition, during the current year she also had used the five days of absence allowed for family care.

Unfortunately, certified teachers for home economics were increasingly unavailable. Other subject-matter teachers had tried to fill in for Elaine during their preparation periods. On occasion, local authorities in the community had served for one day and delivered a related home economics topic to students. Some parental complaints had been received in regard to this practice, and the assistant superintendent for instruction had called the school principal, Pat Allen, about the absentee problem.

Principal Allen sat back in his office chair and thought, "Just what can I do now?"

Question:

Without the use of a "magic wand," assume the role of Principal Allen and set forth your administrative recommendations for resolving this matter. In spite of the limited information available to you regarding funding and the school's personnel situation, give serious thought to the matter herein that is based on an actual case in practice. What, in your opinion, for example, is the first priority in this matter? Students? Elaine Ora's retention? Parental concerns? The central district administrators' concerns? As the school principal, tell us about your administrative actions in this case.

References

Cacio, W. F. (2003). *Managing human resources: Productivity, quality of work life, profits* (6th ed.). New York, NY: McGraw-Hill/Irwin.

Clifford, M., Behrstock-Sherratt, E., & Fetters, J. (2012). *The ripple effect: A synthesis of research on principal influence to inform performance evaluation design. A Quality School Leadership issue brief.* Naperville, IL: American Institutes for Research.

Clifton, D. O., & Nelson, P. (1992). *Soar with your strengths.* New York, NY: Dell.

Concordia University Online. (2013). *Five tips for teacher work-life balance.* Retrieved from http://education.cu-portland.edu/blog/educator-tips/five-tips-for-teacher-work-life-balance

Deadrick, D., & Stone, D. (2009). Emerging trends in human resource management theory and research. *Human Research Management Review, 19*(2), 51–52.

Deibert, J. P., & Hoy, W. F. (1977). "Custodial" high schools and self-actualization of students. *Educational Research Quarterly, 2*(2), 24–31.

Galinsky, E. (2010). *Minds in the making: The seven essential life skills every child needs.* New York, NY: HarperCollins.

Greengard, S. (2012, June 28). *Workforce Management*'s present, past publishers talk HR trends. *Workforce.* Retrieved from http://www.workforce.com/articles/workforce-management-s-present-past-publishers-talk-hr-trends

Heathfield, S. M. (2013). Ten top human resources trends of the decade. *About.com.* Retrieved from http://humanresources.about.com/od/businessmanagement/a/top_ten_trends.htm

Hess, F. M., & Kelly, A. P. (2005). Ready to lead? Today's principals aren't learning the skills they need, these researchers say. *American School Board Journal, 192*(7), 22–25.

Hopkins, W., & Crain, K. (1985). *School climate: The key to an effective school.* Paper presented at the annual meeting of the National Association of School Administrators, New Orleans, LA.

Hoy, W. K., & Appleberry, J. B. (1970). Teacher-principal relationships in 'humanistic' and 'custodial' elementary schools. *Journal of Experimental Education, 39*(2), 27–31.

Lunenburg, F. C. (1983). Pupil control ideology and self-concept as a learner. *Educational Research Quarterly, 8*(3), 33–39.

Norton, M. S. (1987). *Competency-based preparation of educational administrators: Tasks, competencies and indicators of competencies.* Tempe, AZ: Arizona State University.

Norton, M. S. (2008). *Human resources administration for educational leaders.* Thousand Oaks, CA: Sage.

Paredes, V., & Frazer, L. (1992). *School climate in AISD.* Austin, TX: Independent School District, Office of Research and Evaluation.

Schmidt, F. L., & Hunter, J. E. (1998). The validity and utility of selection methods in personnel psychology: Practical and theoretical implications of 85 years of research findings. *Psychological Bulletin, 124*(2), 262–274.

Smith, R. E. (1998). *Human resources administration: A school-based perspective.* Larchmont, NY: Eye on Education.

Webb, L. D., & Norton, M. S. (2009). *Human resources administration: Personnel issues and needs in education* (5th ed.). Upper Saddle River, NJ: Merrill.

Wellins, R. S., Smith, A. B., & Erker, S. (2009). *Nine best practices for effective talent management* [White paper, revised]. Development Dimensions International. Retrieved from https://www.ddiworld.com/DDIWorld/media/white-papers/ninebestpracticetalentmanagement_wp_ddi.pdf?ext=.pdf

Wikipedia. (2013, October 9). Talent management. Retrieved from http://en.wikipedia.org/wiki/Talent-management

Winter, J. S., & Sweeney, J. (1994). Improving school climate: Administrators are key. *NASSP Bulletin, 78*(564), 65–69.

Zeitler, N. A. (2013, August 7). The top 7 trends in HR. *SAP.info.* Retrieved from http://en.sap.info/the-top-7-trends-in-hr/97227

CHAPTER

2

Leadership for Implementing the Human Resources Processes at the Local School Level

Primary chapter goal:

To gain an understanding of the paramount importance of planning and organization in the implementation of each of the primary processes of the human resources function.

Planning and the Human Resources Plan Itself Provide Guidelines for Assessing Human Decisions and Activities of the School

Chapter 1 presented the trending movement of many HR processes from the central district office to the local school under the leadership of the school principal. The chapter also underlined the paramount importance of implementing quality procedures for each of the human resources processes as they relate to the stated goals and objectives of the school. Chapter 2 presents the primary HR processes that must be attended at the local school level. Each of the human resources processes of planning, recruiting, selecting, orienting, assigning, developing and evaluating significantly influence the leadership effectiveness of the school principal.

Visitations and interviews with practicing school principals reveal one major conclusion. The extent to which principals are implementing the HR processes in practice varies widely; the gap between the implementation of

HR processes that should be in practice and the HR processes that are actually being implemented is problematic. For example, in some cases, the school principal has little if anything to do with personnel recruitment, the hiring of support staff, or has limited knowledge of the legal implications of interviewing and hiring practices. We submit that your effectiveness in the administration of the human resources function in your school will determine the overall success of your school leadership. High-quality HR programs are always in evidence in those schools that have high student achievement performance, high teacher retention and positive school climates. The topic of school climate is presented in Chapter 4.

The Human Resources Planning Process: The Foundation for Success

The administration of the local school HR function is a cooperative endeavor between the school district's central HR office and the local school principal. In some instances, the school's assistant principal is delegated the responsibility for overseeing certain processes of the HR function. The ultimate accountability for the results and effectiveness of the school's HR program depends on the leadership of the school principal.

Effective planning and organizing are the end products of the school leader's administrative skills and the results of hard work. Planning is important because it can offset uncertainty and foster positive change. **Planning** involves forecasting, designing, participating, cooperating and collaborating. For example, *forecasting* centers on looking to the future and assessing probabilities. It involves using the results of study and analysis of pertinent data to plan for future events and/or conditions that confront or will confront the school's programs. *Designing* is the creation of plans of action directed toward specific goals and organizational policy. *Participating* necessitates *cooperating* with those individuals that will be involved in the planning process and also those who will be affected by the results of the planning process. In order to achieve the best results, *collaborating* with all possible stakeholders is of paramount importance. It is not simply the organizing of certain committees that will report back their ideas on one particular problem or program provision. It is not the establishment of the school's or the school system's vision statements without the follow-up procedures for implementing specific goals and objectives and administering and evaluating the goals and objectives set forth. Nor is a plan a public relations announcement that the school is completing a year-long study of programs and operations that seems to fade away until it's time to do another study.

Perhaps Young (2008) said it best: "Planning is a methodological mechanism for projecting intentions and actions rather than reacting to causes and events impacting education and the schooling process" (p. 62). This definition fits the purposes of planning in the HR function in schools. The definition suggests a thoughtful process for guiding and projecting administrative decisions as the school principal and staff go about determining the school's personnel needs and meeting them in an effective manner.

Hanlon (1968) spoke of the most difficult but important part of planning, conceptualizing the plan of the work. He used the idea of artist Leonardo da Vinci "that the execution of the work of art is the easiest part of the artist's job, while the most difficult part is the conception and composition of the work" (p. 29). It makes little difference what strokes of the artist's brush are used without the conception and plan because none results in a better painting than any other. Hanlon underscores the crux of this point by noting that the conception of the plan and the plan itself provide the guidelines for assessing the decisions and activities of the personnel in the organization in terms of what they envision the organization to be in the future. You must always keep in mind that the HR function is a planned function. Without the foundation that planning provides, what is done is most likely to be directionless and will miss stated purposes.

The Knowledge and Skills You Need for Effective Strategic Planning

Some authorities argue that merely attempting to prepare for the future falls short of the desirable ends. Rather, as Goodstein et al. (1986) point out, the process of strategic planning enables the organization to help change its own future, as opposed to simply preparing for future needs and changes. Strategic planning is necessary at the local school level because the economic conditions, learner needs and expectations, and many other environmental factors will not be the same two, five or ten years from now as they are today. Strategic planning is not necessarily the making of future decisions; rather it is focused upon current planning decisions about what you must do now to realize desired outcomes in the future. Strategic planning helps you deal with the inevitability of change; it encourages the implementation of effective administration.

There are at least six basic elements related to a strategic plan (Baird et al., 1983):

1. The educational environment—an internal and external scan of the educational environment and the culture of the school system to determine the many considerations that can be viewed simultaneously as constraints

and opportunities. To know the community always has been a basic responsibility of the school principal.

2. The mission statement of the school system—developing a clear vision of the priority goals and objectives of the total organization is vital for guiding the planning process.
3. The implementation of the school system's strategic plan—this is crucial, as a plan without implementation is meaningless.
4. The development and implementation of the strategy plans for the individual schools in the school system—tying the school's strategic plan to the school system's plan in terms of budgeting, curriculum, personnel and pupil services.
5. Examining, analyzing and assessing the results of each school's strategic plan with that of the school system's plan—making necessary adjustments in the system's strategic plan and the plans of local schools as the analyses results suggest.
6. Reaching the goal of the school's and school system's integrated mission strategies—individual unit plans must be tied to the organization's strategic objectives. As Goetz (1949) points out, plans by themselves are dormant ideas. On the other hand, administrative actions that are not based on effective planning most likely will result in chaos.

Operational Planning at the School Level: Your Key to Successful HR Results

Each department, unit and division within the school must develop an operational plan. Operational plans for the human resources function in the school must tie to the guiding strategic plan of the school and in turn to the overall strategic plan of the school system. An operational plan is tied to one or more of the strategic objectives. Thus each operational plan contributes to the achievement of a strategic objective. When several departments have an operational plan that contributes to the overall school's strategic plan, it serves to provide a focus on school-wide priorities. For example, if a school's strategic objective was to improve school safety for students and staff, the curriculum unit might design a special unit on school safety practices, the central office might work cooperatively with local police and fire departments to design improved safety measures inside and outside the school building, and the physical/recreation unit might work to decrease injuries in physical sports and education facilities.

Operational plans commonly include the primary goals that serve to guide directions for operational procedures. The goals establish the ends to be sought, procedures to be followed, appropriate timelines for goal completion as fit the case, methods for monitoring procedures and assessments to be utilized for measuring results.

Since the needs of students and personnel differ from school to school, operational plans will differ according to these conditions. One school might be focused on improving student achievement in math and science and another on reading. Thus, the professional staff mix will differ from school to school or within the school as well. Strategies for utilizing the talents of personnel will change as the priorities in the operational plan changes. Staff utilization looms important.

Historically, school principals have not been directly involved in policy development; that has been the responsibility of the school board. Administrative regulation development, in turn, has been delegated to the superintendent of schools and central district office staff. Principals have been responsible for the implementation of the district's policies and regulations, and have been concerned primarily with the adoption of certain rules and regulations that pertain to a particular school's procedures. This historical arrangement, although still in operation for the most part, has moved gradually downward to the school superintendent and now to the school principal. The primary evidence of this move is exemplified by the movement of site-based management whereby local school councils establish some "policy matters" and recommend school regulations as well.

Operational planning at the school level results in several benefits for the school principal. As previously noted, it serves as an effective correlate with the school's strategic plan and it provides information data to support changes/improvements in personnel, policies and regulations, and processes for recruiting, selecting, developing and compensating human resources in the school.

The Recruitment Process: A Key to Goal Achievement

Recruitment of personnel remains the primary responsibility of the school district's central HR office. Nevertheless, important opportunities to recruit quality personnel are initiated by the school principal and members of the local school faculty. The school principal can capitalize on finding talented personnel by frequently seeking the recommendations of the school's professional and support members. Tied closely to the recruitment activities is the process of re-recruitment of talent presently on the school's faculty. Re-recruitment is discussed later in the chapter.

Technological communication has entered into the recruitment process in business and industry and now is finding its way into the recruitment process in education.

> The decade has brought about the transforming of employee recruiting and social and media interaction and networking. . . . Employers have seen a transformation in how people find each other for networking and jobs this decade . . . from networking on discussion sites such as LinkedIn, Facebook, Twitter, and Ecademy, networking and recruiting will never be the same again.
>
> (Heathfield, 2013)

In addition, there is a growing number of recruiting services online. Empirical evidence reveals wide differences in the effectiveness of online recruitment. Some commercial advertisements of recruitment show long lists of endorsements by users of the service. We recommend that you investigate such services thoroughly before getting involved with them. Checking with reliable others that have had experience with a job-seekers' service is wise. It is not the purpose here to detail the pluses and minuses of online services, but such differences do exist. For example, although the Internet service does provide access to an ample number of potential applicants, the competition for the same applicants can be nationwide.

Historically, HR recruitment and selection activities have taken a large reduction in the total needs of employees (RIF) due to a variety of reasons, from declining enrollments, school consolidations, financial shortfalls and curriculum changes to problematic teacher shortages due to enrollment increases, pushes for increased emphasis on subject offerings such as physical education, reading, mathematics/science, and special swings from education, and foreign languages. Both the RIF process and the need to recruit new personnel require the implementation of effective personnel administration on the part of the school principal.

Guidelines for Implementing a Successful Recruitment Process

Guidelines are valuable directives for calling the principal's attention to common steps for implementing a particular procedure. That is, guidelines help the principal to stop and think about important steps in the planning, organizing and implementation of the recruitment process, and cause him or her to ask just how the guidelines can serve in the implementation of the HR process at hand.

Recruitment Planning—as previously mentioned in this chapter, planning is the process of determining the purposes, intentions and results of what the process wants to accomplish. In personnel planning, the purpose focuses on developing a pool of applicants who are best qualified to meet the position needs of a specific teaching or support position. Planning necessitates decisions relative to the organization of qualified recruitment teams and informing them of school and school district policies and regulations related to employee recruitment. For example, does the policy suggest that recruitment should be carried out on a broad basis or that staff balance relative to experience, gender and personal interests would be considered? Recruitment goals and purposes stem directly from school-board policies and the school district's administrative regulations. Site-based councils commonly request involvement in personnel recruitment. We recommend that any such involvement by council members be centered on purposes to be achieved rather than how the process is to be administered by the school principal and the professional staff.

Organizing for Recruitment at the Local School Level: Why Is It Essential?

Successful recruitment, like any other administrative activity, depends largely on the extent that it is effectively organized. Most persons would agree that the position requirements for the hiring of a sixth-grade teacher or the hiring of a social studies teacher would differ from one school to another. Activities in the recruitment process include position analyses and position descriptions, establishing the recruitment pool, controlling the recruitment process and implementing the re-recruitment of personnel.

A position analysis is a scientific examination of a position in order to determine its makeup relative to its specific tasks, responsibilities and constituent parts. It includes information about the position itself; the qualifications required; schedule of activities and time requirements; effects of the work on the employee in terms of relationships, stress, safety, peer/student/parent relationships; conditions of the work in terms of workload and environment; and requirements of relationships within the school, the school district and the school community.

It is true that position analysis is most commonly associated with positions of support personnel (e.g., secretarial staff, maintenance workers, service personnel). However, a position analysis for teaching positions has several important benefits for both the school principal and the school teacher, including the tying of the position to the school's goals and objectives, serving as a basis for recruitment and selection of personnel, identifying areas of importance for staff growth and development, providing special safety provisions, identifying the effects of the position on the employee, stating the position's relationships with the community, underscoring personnel performance evaluation criteria and others.

One might say that, "We don't do position analyses or position descriptions at the local school level, these things are done at the central district office." What should be asked is, "How might position analyses and position descriptions for employee positions in our school be of special benefit concerning our school purposes?" The time and effort put forth in developing position analyses and position descriptions go far in helping to assure the effective implementation of all HR processes.

Position Descriptions and Their Many Purposes

Position descriptions are developed from the previous work of position analysis. A position description is a written statement that presents the position's important tasks and related responsibilities. Position descriptions are especially valuable to the school principal, the potential position holder and the present position holder. When recommended by the school principal and school superintendent, and then approved by the school board, position descriptions become important legal documents as well.

Position descriptions commonly include the position title and qualifications, the position of the immediate supervisor, the persons to be supervised, the position goal, position responsibilities, special knowledge and skills required, terms of employment and performance evaluation procedures. Just hoping that the candidate for the position has these traits and characteristics will not suffice. Later we discuss just how such qualities can be assessed.

Position descriptions are of special value in determining interview questions. For example, assume that the special knowledge and skills section of the position description stated that, "Specific skills related to human relations, judgment, problem analysis ability, written and oral communication, decision making, planning and organization, and leadership are important for effectiveness in the position." It is clear that questions asked and other ways of assessing such factors as judgment, decision-making and leadership would need to be developed and utilized in the interviewing procedures.

Recruitment Sources: Without Which Not!

Recruitment sources are often developed through past experience. In some cases walk-ins constitute the majority of applicants that form the recruitment pool. A local or nearby higher education institution that has developed a cooperative teacher internship program with the school is another viable recruitment resource. Recruitment sources often change due to the influencing factors of competition for staff personnel, special program needs, supply and demand, and other economic factors. However, university/college placement offices, job fairs, advertising in newspapers or even in movie theaters, and other media are among the ongoing recruitment sources utilized by many schools and school districts. Although the Web has received increasing use as a recruitment resource, the principal faces both pro and con results regarding its favorableness. For example, although the Web is a ready source for potential applicants, it is widely available to other recruiters on a national basis; competition is problematic.

Social media currently are receiving considerable attention as the contemporary resource for contacting position applicants. As previously mentioned, Facebook, LinkedIn, Twitter and other social-networking sources are being utilized by business and industry for recruiting purposes, and education is not far behind.

Strategies for Establishing the Recruitment Pool

A recruitment pool consists of applicants that have passed initial screening on the basis of information gathered through the position application, recruitment interviews, conference calls, references, college transcripts and certification checks. One common screening procedure is the use of a brief telephone interview. For example, oral communication can be assessed in this procedure, as well as information gained by asking questions such as, "What instructional methods have you found to be most effective in regard to student discipline?" or "What extracurricular programs and/or activities are of special interest to you?"

Some schools do not have the advantage of having immediate sources for recruitment close to an institution with a teacher-training program, or perhaps they do not have the reputation of being in a high-performing school district. In this case, the school might have to implement special strategies to attract qualified applicants. For example, the school might consider giving special attention to retaining talented teachers, encouraging retired teachers to return to the classroom, or guaranteeing each prospective applicant an interview if they do apply. Some schools use the strategy of sending their best teachers to do the recruitment interviews at teacher-placement offices or to job fairs where they show photographs of the school's students and staff at work and the instructional facilities available at the school.

Potential Recruitment Sources: Your Recruitment Successes Will Pinpoint Best Contacts

The following listing includes most of the common sources available for establishing a quality applicant pool. We do understand that central HR offices often take the primary responsibility for establishing applicant pools for all schools in the school district. However, the recruitment process is also one of the HR processes that has been gradually delegated to the local school principal. Which of the following sources are readily available to you?

Recruitment Sources

1. Online Web
2. Placement Bureaus, Job Hotlines
3. Job Fairs/Roundups (instate/outstate)
4. FTA Chapters
5. Media/Newspapers
6. Internal Faculty Referrals
7. Local Talent, Ex-Teachers
8. Employment Agencies (instate/outstate)
9. Student Teachers
10. Networking with Other School Principals
11. University Teachers
12. Teachers Associations
13. Employment Agencies
14. Teachers Aids/Grow Your Own
15. Walk-Ins, Call-Ins
16. College Recruiting
17. Professional Journals
18. Job Postings—Multiple
19. Word Of Mouth
20. Mailing Sources
21. Re-Recruitment Efforts

Let's Retain Our Quality Personnel: Increasing Teacher Retention Through Re-Recruitment Activities

Most everyone is aware of the statistics regarding teacher retention in education. Studies continue to reveal that teaching personnel are leaving the profession at the rate of 50 percent after a five-year period. Turnover among teachers is itself only a symptom of other causal factors that lead to teacher loss. School principals must take the lead in implementing strategies that serve to keep talented teaching personnel on the job. The solution does not rest simply in given them more money. Salpeter (2003) supported a statement by the National Commission on Teaching and America's Future that "contrary to popular belief, the main challenge facing schools in their quest for qualified teachers is not recruiting, but retention." The key to keeping good teachers was effective staff development.

Perhaps the best practices that have given the best results for teacher retention are summarized as follows:

- Capitalizing on the individual's primary strengths and interests. Teachers, like employees in other professions, have the highest job satisfaction when they are able to apply their personal talents to their daily work. Some principals utilize a brief questionnaire at mid-year and toward the end of the school year that asks for information relative to the teacher's interest in teaching assignments and requested changes, if any. One part of the questionnaire asks the teacher about their interest in extracurricular assignments and the individual's suggestions for assignments in this area for the forthcoming year. In some cases, a teacher might be reluctant to suggest that he or she is qualified for a certain assignment. In these cases, the principal can take the lead in suggesting a new challenge that brings about a variety of experiences and new interests for the teacher.
- Confirming your appreciation of the individual's important contributions to the implementation and realization of the school's mission, its goals and objectives. Every employee wants to know how well he or she is doing their job, even when they believe that they are doing it well. Recall the story of Amelia set forth in Chapter 1. When Dr. Randall confirmed the fact that she was an excellent teacher, the result was a feeling of worth and job satisfaction.
- Help each employee develop a plan of personal and professional growth and development. Bathhurst (2007) reported that the single most important factor in the fostering of job satisfaction is the opportunities available for personal growth and development in the area of an individual's career

development. The topic of professional development is discussed further in Chapter 3. One school principal knew of Keith Powell's interest in school finance and accounting. The principal asked Keith if he might give him some help on certain procedures relative to the forthcoming school budget requirements. Keith more than welcomed the opportunity to participate. Such involvement provided him an opportunity for continuous learning in an area of personal interest. The school benefited by Keith's contributions, but Keith learned a great deal about the school's budgeting requirements, policy and legal requirements, and asked if he might participate in the budget process again next year, a win-win cooperative activity.

- Primary considerations for implementing re-recruitment activities. When it comes to re-recruitment leadership, you know that one's feeling of belonging and security on the job looms important. As was illustrated by the best practice example of Mary Dearell in Chapter 1, when she became reunited with important work in the school that was appreciated by all, her feeling of being a part of the school and the accomplishment of its mission increased, and she was once again motivated.

The Human Resources Selection Process: A Key to School Success

Once a viable pool of applicants is accomplished, the selection process is your next human resources task; perhaps it is the most important. One of the most effective ways to make important program improvements in your school is through an effective selection process. School principals often comment that hiring is their most important job. A problem hire leaves a long trail. The time spent in dealing with an individual that is a bad fit for the school will consume more of your time than otherwise would be spent in implementing an effective selection process.

An effective employee selection process consists of several specific activities. You have already completed the first selection activity through the recruitment activities discussed previously. For example, you now have on hand the material gathered during the recruitment process (e.g., application information, certification verifications, experience information, references, college transcripts, interview results, etc.). This information should be thoroughly reviewed by you and others who will participate in the selection process. Those individuals in the applicant pool that are chosen for further consideration are placed in the candidate pool. Unless you gather and analyze such information, your candidate selections are likely to be based on subjective traits rather than on objective data.

Implementing Selection Interviews

Next, the candidates that have been determined to be the best fit for the position to be filled should be contacted about their present interest in the position opening and, if still available, a position interview is scheduled. Persons that are involved in the interviewing activity must be trained in the process. An interview guide that serves to focus on gathering information that relates to the position requirements should be developed for use by interviewers, especially when multiple interviews are utilized. In most cases, each interviewer asks the same questions. Such a procedure provides consistency to the selection process and can reduce the judgmental opinions that often enter into interview appraisals.

Avoiding Problems in the Interview Process

Questions that can and cannot be asked of an interviewee can be troublesome. Giving advice on what questions school principals cannot ask in interview sessions with candidates is somewhat like walking a tightrope; one mistake and you could be in trouble. In practice, there sometimes is a very small difference between an okay question and one that is not legal. The Age Discrimination in Employment Act of 1967 sets forth the guidelines for dealing with the age questions in hiring personnel.

One tip that looms important in the matter of interview questions: Be certain that the questions asked pertain directly to the qualifications required for the position opening in question. For example, it is not legal to ask questions relating to an individual's disabilities. However, such a question might be okay if it pertains specifically to the qualifications necessary for doing the job. That is, if the job description requires heavy lifting, it most likely would be permissible to point out that the work did require such competency. A second tip is about questions dealing with race, color, sex, religion, national origin, age, and yes, disability, marital status, family status, future plans for children, childcare accommodations, sexual orientation, gender, and pregnancy status. Avoid any question in these categories with the intent to use the answer for making a hiring decision.

Empirical evidence and authorities in the area of discrimination point out many questions that are indeed illegal to ask, but have related questions that are legal since they pertain to job or occupational qualifications. For example, it is illegal to ask a question that asks for the candidate's national origin, but alright to ask if he or she is legally authorized to work in the United States as a basis for hiring. The question, "What religious holidays do you celebrate" is not legal. However, it is okay to ask, "Are you able to work on Sundays?" And, it is not legal to ask, "Is English your first language?" but permissible to ask, "What other languages do you speak?" According to empirical practice, it is not permissible to ask, "Have you ever been arrested?" but it is permissible to ask, "Have you ever been convicted of a crime?" The matter of the interviewer asking the interviewee for permission to get his or her credit history has been troublesome in many interview sessions. However, this question appears to be permissible if it pertains to the work qualifications in some manner. One story is told of the interviewer that was intrigued by the "beauty" of the interviewee's last name and asked the history of its derivation. The interviewer caught herself asking a probable national origin question and said, "You don't have to answer that question if you do not want to do so."

In summary, always be certain that your questions in an interview have specific relationship to the qualifications of the position in question and proceed cautiously before asking any questions of the no-no variety: race, color, national origin, age, religion, sex and others.

The Type of Interview Should Fit the Case

Behavior interviews commonly focus on four dimensions:

1. Knowledge of the curriculum for the grade level or subject area (degrees, GPAs, grade or subject knowledge);
2. Experience and preparation (experience in the area of the position of application, memberships in professional organizations, workshops or other development activities);
3. Professional characteristics and qualifications (poise and stability, oral communication qualities, personality/sensitivity, leadership traits, such as judgment, goal orientation, understanding of student learning); and
4. Synthesis (summary assessments relative to candidate's overall qualifications).

Telephone interviews can save time and also serve as important screening tools. Telephone interviews can be brief, and yet the interviewer can gain important information relative to such factors as oral communication or specific responses by asking a question such as, "What teaching methods seem to work best for you in the classroom?" or "If a particular student is falling behind in the class work, what steps would you take to get the student back on track?"

On the basis of the telephone interview or a comparable personal interview, a more detailed selection interview is appropriate. In some instances, a **performance interview** is conducted. For example, a candidate for a primary grade teaching position might be asked to "teach us a reading lesson in the use of phonics" or a middle school mathematics candidate might be asked to "teach us how you would introduce the concept of the Pythagorean theorem to grade seven students." The interview guide mentioned in the previous section would provide clues to the interview criteria to be observed. Knowledge of the subject might not be the focus of the performance results at all. Such factors as stress tolerance, oral communication, poise, and personal performance might be the interview criteria being appraised.

School principals and selection teams must decide in advance the interview technique(s) to be used and the important characteristics to be addressed in the selection process. The best interview is the one that provides the candidate's qualifications relative to the knowledge/skills/traits set forth in the position description. Although we recommend that the "pat" questions (such as "what are your strengths and weaknesses,") be avoided, we do recommend that you instead ask the interviewee to tell you about a time he or she was especially successful in working with a gifted or marginal student, or served as a student advocate in a difficult situation.

Although we favor advance research and preparation before the interview and the use of an interview guide, this does not set aside the opportunity to push for details when the interviewee is not specific in giving an important answer about such matters as gaps in work experience or frequent changes in work positions. In any case, you have the responsibility of determining if the candidate being interviewed is indeed the best choice for the position in question. Background checks today are expected in all cases. We also favor interview training for all persons doing the school interviews. Such training should include information concerning what practices are not legal and/or are improper. In the end, ask yourself, did the interview result in providing the information that was sought by the interview plan?

What Characteristics of Teacher Candidates Are Viewed as Being Most Important?

Kowalski et al. (1992, pp. 34–38) studied the characteristics for teacher selection that school principals themselves considered to be of most importance. Figure 2.1 shows the results of the principals' selections on a rating scale of 1 (low) and 5 (high).

Characteristic	Mean Score 1–low and 5–high
1. Respect for students	4.94
2. Honesty	4.88
3. Ability to work with peers	4.80
4. Verbal communication	4.79
5. Quality of previous experience	4.79
6. Emotional stability	4.69
7. Commitment to the teaching profession	4.69
8. Professional commitment	4.69
9. Ability to assess pupil progress	4.69
10. Professional pride	4.60
11. Willingness to be a team player	4.58
12. Effective discipline	4.54
13. Written communication	4.54
14. Ability to retain confidentiality	4.53
15. Knowledge of child growth and development	4.47

FIGURE 2.1. Important Characteristics for Teacher Selection as Viewed by Principals

Preparing Candidate Nominations and Reporting to the Proper Offices of the School District

Submission of your final candidate selections commonly are submitted to the director of human resources for the school district, the school superintendent, or other school official as fits the case. It is a common practice that the superintendent of schools presents the recommended listing for hiring. Although the competition for quality personnel has brought about the need to offer a candidate a job prior to the school board's approval action, it must be made clear to the candidate that official hiring is contingent on the official approval of the school board. Even an oral contract given to a candidate is binding if, indeed, it meets the criteria that define a contract. To be binding, a contract must have been agreed upon by both parties, the considerations of the contract must be valid and must deal with legal subject matter and definite terms, and the two parties involved must be competent.

Check How Well You Are Doing: Assessing Selection Outcomes

Accountability necessitates the analysis and assessment of program outcomes. The HR processes of recruitment and selection are reflected in the performance outcomes of those individuals ultimately hired. Thus, performance appraisals serve as hard data for assessing the results of hiring judgments and procedures.

School climate measures provide evidence of the human qualities of persons that you hired. How many of the teachers hired remain on the faculty after one year, two years, three years or more? Although teachers leave a school for various reasons, hires that were bad fits for the school make it necessary for the principal to review selection procedures. An inadequate induction program might be one cause of employee turnover. The HR processes of induction, assignment, stability and performance appraisal are discussed in the following sections of the chapter.

Snapshot 1

Tyler Patrick was first-year math hire at Whittier High School. During reporting week at the outset of the school year, Tyler arrived early at the school office and was greeted by the school principal, Dylan Andrews.

"Come with me, Tyler. I want you to meet Jake Valentiner, who will be serving as your helping teacher this semester. We have used helping teachers for several years as individuals that will be available to answer questions that you might have and so forth."

Tyler followed the principal down the hall and into the room of Mr. Valentiner.

"Jake," said Mr. Andrews, "this is Tyler Patrick. You probably met him when he came to the school for the group interview."

Tyler and Jake shook hands and exchanged greetings.

"I'll leave the two of you alone and you can get acquainted," said the principal. "I'll see you both this afternoon at our staff social."

"Well," said Jake, "I will be glad to help you in any way that I can. Just remember, if you have any questions about where things are or how things are done, just let me know. Perhaps we can talk again later at the social get-together this afternoon."

Tyler thanked Jake, left the room and went up to his own room on the second floor. He thought to himself, "I guess this is it. I wonder if the class textbooks are in that back closet or if students get books some other way? I really don't feel comfortable running back up to Mr. Valentiner to find out."

Think about it. Do you remember your orientation at the time of your first teaching position? Was your orientation similar to Tyler Patrick's, or was it an effective process that served to provide you the information needed for a successful start that led to a successful school year for you? We want you to think about what constitutes an effective orientation, and we discuss this HR process in the following section.

The Orientation Process: Helping Teachers and Staff Get Off to a Successful Start

More than 40 years ago, a study by Berglas (1973) found that personal assistance given to new teachers in an induction program was the single most important factor in enhancing school climate relative to teacher morale. The process of assisting newly assigned personnel as they adjust to their given work assignment in the school in ways that give them the confidence to apply their talents toward the accomplishment of their responsibilities is termed **induction**, or more recently, **orientation**. Orientation load formulas such as the Douglass load formula or the Norton/Bria formula (Norton, 2008) for measuring elementary school teacher load give the principal a reliable tool for bringing about equity of load among the teaching staff. In some cases, the principal might want to reduce the workload of a new teacher by not assigning them to extracurricular activities, or perhaps by having them teach one less class than others at the secondary school level. At the elementary school level, extracurricular duties could be lightened for all newly assigned personnel that enter your school. Orientation procedures first and foremost should be based on the new employee's needs and interests. How do you know the employee's needs and interests? You ask them. The orientation process will differ for employees that are new to the teaching profession, new to the school district, or new to your school and their school assignment.

Helping the New Employee Toward a Successful Year

Human resources processes are interrelated. The recruitment and selection processes, for example, serve as initiatory orientation activities, in that they commonly include information about the school community, the school's mission and some of the special services available to teachers. **Orientation** includes those procedures and activities implemented by the school leadership to meet the needs of employees new to the school, and re-emphasize the culture of the school and its mission and purposes. Orientation, then, begins at the outset of the employee's application for position and continues throughout the hiring process for just as long as the employee and/or the school principal view it as necessary. Figure 2.2 illustrates the general procedures and interrelationships of various HR activities that facilitate the teacher's personal and professional development and enhance their interest in remaining with the school.

Position Application → Selected for Applicant Pool → Chosen for Candidate Pool → Hired as a New Teacher → Orientation → Mentoring/Coaching → Professional Development → Talent Management → TEACHER RETENTION

FIGURE 2.2. HR Activities and Their Interrelationships

An effective orientation process provides answers to the common questions of new teachers who have common concerns about:

- the instructional resources available to the teacher for use in the classroom;
- homework rules in terms of student time expectations;
- student discipline expectations, including student tardies and absences;
- parental communication and visitation requirements;
- student grading procedures and retention and/or student failure procedures;
- personal absence reporting procedures;
- resources available relative to personal safety, health care, and financial aid;
- relationships with other school district personnel.

Position Assignment: Matching the Person to the Position

Don't make the mistake of hiring a talented person and thinking that they will do fine even if the position of placement is not really the best. Such a move represents the first step toward job dissatisfaction and thoughts of leaving the position at the earliest possible time. This doesn't mean that a candidate new to teaching and new to an assignment cannot be asked if they will agree to teach grade 6 rather than grade 3, where he or she did their practice teaching. In fact, empirical evidence suggests that a teacher that is assigned to a grade other than the one of his or her practice teaching will generally want to continue teaching in that grade the following year. However, keep in mind that a new teacher that signs a contract stating that her assignment will be to teach in grade 1 cannot be made to teach another grade; if the contract states that the teacher is to teach mathematics and science, he or she cannot be made to teach social studies (Peterson et al., 1978, pp. 428–429).

An appropriate position placement is one in which the individual is assigned to a subject and/or grade level that coincides with his or her personal interests and strengths. Proper position assignment encourages positive job satisfaction and a healthy school climate, and promotes the individual's intentions of remaining on the school's faculty. When making position assignments, the principal must give careful consideration to:

1. the position description that outlines the specifics of the position in terms of its purposes;
2. the professional competencies required in the role;
3. the preparation and qualities of the person being considered for the assignment;
4. how the assignment lends to the personal interests and strengths of the individual; and
5. how the position will motivate the individual toward a program of continued growth and development.

Empirical evidence and research have supported the contention that having opportunities for professional development ranks high on the list of factors that foster positive job satisfaction.

Working Conditions Loom Important: Providing Equitable Work Assignments

You have done a fine job when you have matched teachers and support personnel to appropriate position assignments. As we have stressed throughout this chapter, employees who have been appropriately assigned will demonstrate higher levels of job satisfaction and instructional performance. Everyone benefits. The new teacher benefits, the school administration benefits, the school district benefits, and, especially, the students will benefit.

One factor of paramount importance is that of knowing the real workload of each teacher. Most professionals would agree with the statements that a new teacher's workload should be carefully assigned. The enthusiasm of new teachers might lead them to accept added assignments that tend to reduce their overall effectiveness. Research studies of teacher load commonly reveal that new teachers often carry the highest teacher load (Norton, 2008). Another caution relates to overloading the most talented personnel on the staff. Without due consideration to using available methods for measuring teacher load, inequities in workload will be evidenced, and those teachers most qualified to contribute to a quality instructional program become overburdened and their work efforts frequently are reduced to a level of mediocrity (Norton, 2008).

When it comes to such matters as work assignments, the effective school principal needs to look to the research in an effort to find more scientific ways to determine teacher workload. For example, which one of the two teachers at Wymore High School (below) is carrying the heaviest teacher load? Read each teacher's assignment and then write down your opinion as to which teacher is carrying the heaviest workload index or if both loads are equal. Then, check the teacher load measurement of each teacher according to the Douglass Teacher Load Formula (Norton, 2008).

Teacher A—High School Mathematics Teacher

Teaching assignments:

2 classes of 10th-grade plane geometry with 21 and 15 students. Each class meets five times a week, class periods are 60 minutes. The two classes have similar students, so one class is considered to be a duplicate.

2 classes of 10th-grade algebra 1 with 25 and 19 students. Each class meets five times a week; class periods are 60 minutes. Classes are not considered to be duplicates.

1 class of 11th-grade algebra 2 with 19 students. The class meets five times a week; class periods are 60 minutes.

Teacher spends an average of 230 minutes per week on non-teaching duties during the semester.

Teacher B—High School English and Social Studies Teacher

Teaching Assignments:

2 classes of 10th-grade American history with 15 and 22 students. Each class meets five times a week for 50 minutes. Classes are considered to be duplicates.

2 classes of 11th–12th-grade world history with 21 and 32 students. Each class meets five times a week for 50 minutes. Classes are not considered to be duplicates.

1 class of 12th-grade Civics with 18 students. The class meets five times a week for 50 minutes.

Teacher spends an average of 460 minutes per week as sponsor of the Civics Club and member of the school district's social studies curriculum committee.

If your selection for heaviest workload was teacher B, you were correct. How did you arrive at your answer? Was it just a lucky guess? Did you think that the course subjects of one of the teachers were more difficult than the other teacher? According to the Douglass high school teacher load formula, teacher A had a load index of 28.05 and teacher B a load index of 32.09. The Douglass formula does not tell us how many hours a teacher is working; rather, it provides a load index for each teacher in the school that can be compared and then used to make adjustments when inequities are found in the workload assignments. The mean load index for teachers in the school can be calculated, and loads above and below the average can be examined. For example, the load indices for all of the teaching staff can be examined and considered when extracurricular duties are assigned. It is not uncommon to find that the workload of a teacher is twice the load of another teacher in the same school, and it is not planned to be that way. The point is that as school principal, you need hard data for controlling position assignments and working for equity among teacher workloads.

Snapshot 2—Oh, No, Not Another Class to Teach!

Principal Miller was being pressed by the fact that more than 30 students were not able to enroll in the middle school's beginning vocal music class, and both the students and parents in grade 10 had voiced complaints about the matter. The music teacher, Greg Stephens, was teaching three different classes of vocal music and was the sponsor of the music club that met once a month after school.

Principal Miller asked Greg to meet him during his preparation period on Thursday to discuss this situation.

"Come on in," said Principal Miller as he approached the office door. "Have a seat. I wanted to visit with you about our need to add a new beginning vocal music class for next semester that begins next month. We have a waiting list for this class and the site-based council members have asked me to see what can be done about this problem. As you are well aware, you are carrying a four-class load and our common workload for teachers is five classes each semester. I do realize that you have been sponsoring the music club after school once a month. I want to ask you to take on this new class."

"Oh, no," responded Greg. "I am already overloaded. I have accepted vocal presentations by the Lions Club and several parent–teacher groups during this semester, along with taking the advanced music class members to the October Festival to perform just recently. Then there is my modern jazz group that has been invited to several special wedding and birthday events. I just can't take on any more assignments."

Principal Miller reached for some papers on his desk and stated, "Look here, Greg, first of all, I do appreciate your community music contributions. But my calculations of the workload for all our staff members place your index in the bottom quartile. As you can see, your teaching load for actual classroom instruction is only 19.6, but what we call your cooperative load is among the highest indices at 19.8. Of course, the greatest demands on your cooperative load are created primarily by your personal willingness to do a great deal of performing for outside-of-school events."

Greg sat back in his chair and was quiet for a time. "You know," said Greg, "I am the one creating my high workload. The figures show that I just have to start saying 'no' more often. If I reduce some community programs, I can indeed spend more time with our own students that want to sing."

Snapshot 2 illustrates the fact that teachers are professionals and want to do what is best. Principal Miller was able to show Greg that his present workload was being initiated primarily by his acceptance of invitations outside the school. Unless you, as principal, are able to demonstrate the facts of workload problems, either inequities will continue or you most likely will be viewed as being unfair in making assignments. An illustration of the Douglass Teacher Load Formula and the Norton/Bria Formula for Measuring Elementary School Teacher Load will be presented at the end of this chapter.

How the Principal Can Maintain a Viable Workforce: Human Resources Leadership at Its Best

Personnel authorities in the field are saying that one of the top three personnel challenges within the next decade is that of retaining and rewarding employees (SHRM, 2012). If there were a surefire plan for maintaining a viable work force, the problems of teacher retention, assisting marginal teachers, teacher absenteeism and dealing with troubled employees would have been resolved years ago. It isn't that educational leaders have not worked diligently to maintain stability in the school staffing, but problems relating to working with troubled employees, helping marginal teachers, dealing with conflict and controversy, and trying to reduce teacher turnover still exist.

High teacher turnover in a school is not only costly monetarily, but is also damaging to the continuity of school programming. Although professionals and researchers point out that we have not learned just how to reduce teacher attrition, if a school is experiencing high turnover it is unreasonable to just keep doing the same thing. Other interventions and/or provisions to reduce the problem of retention should be decided and implemented.

The following sections discuss the foregoing problems that face the school leader, and address the needed provisions and describe best practices that have been implemented by some school leaders.

The Influence of School Administrators on Teacher Retention: What the Research Says

The Alliance for Excellent Education (2008) points out that approximately a half million teachers leave their schools each year and only 16 percent of this attrition is due to teacher retirement. Boyd et al. (2011) completed a comprehensive study on the influence of school administrators on teacher retention that was reported in an article published in the *American Educational Research Journal*. The key finding of this study was that teachers' perceptions of the school administration have by far the greatest influence on teacher retention decisions. Lack of support from administrators outranked eleven other aspects of the job by a large margin as a factor for teachers leaving or considering leaving their jobs. Forty-two percent of the study participants ranked lack of support from administrators as the decision factor for leaving.

Most every study of teacher retention concludes that the support of administrators is of paramount importance in retention decisions by teachers. Administrative support commonly is viewed as assisting teachers in their classroom performance, providing challenging opportunities for teachers to experience professional growth and development, being a principal that is viewed as a teacher advocate and doing things that make the teacher's work more enjoyable. Student behavior ranked second most influential with a response of approximately 18 percent. District policy, teaching philosophy, teaching assignment, school safety, emphasis on student testing, ability to help students, respect from students/parents, school facilities, autonomy over the classroom and colleagues fell far behind the factor of lack of administrator support as reasons for not remaining at the school. District policy, for example, received only a 5 percent response as a negative factor, and colleague relations received the smallest response of approximately 2 percent.

Job Satisfaction: Why Your Support Looms Important

The foregoing paragraph carries one of the most important messages in this book, for it underscores the theme of the book: the school principal as a human resources leader. Nevertheless, Boyd et al. (2011) are quick to point out that while their study does provide evidence that the school administration is an important factor in teacher retention decisions, "our data do not provide enough 'richness' about the role of the administration to determine how and why administrative support affects teachers, nor do the data allow us to identify clear policy levers for reform" (p. 27).

We do have important empirical evidence that suggests activities that should be performed in order to improve job satisfaction for reducing the loss of staff. As Young (2008) points out, most employees want information about job expectations and the services that are available to help them meet them. If this kind of information is not provided at the outset of the selection process and continued during orientation and assignment activities, the employee's ability to commit to the school and its goals and objectives is unlikely to occur.

Often heard among staff personnel is the phrase, "One never knows where they stand with the principal." The school principal must realize that all personnel benefit by employees knowing just how their position fits with the school and the commitments and obligations necessary for meeting the requirements. The HR processes of recruitment, selection, assignment, orientation and performance appraisal all can contribute to the employee's understanding of the school district's mission and the school's goals and objectives. "Principals also affect the instructional quality of schools through the recruitment, development, and retention of teachers" (Harris et al., 2010, as cited in Boyd et al., 2011).

Principals need to know which teachers are leaving the school and why. Research studies have found that younger and older teachers have higher turnover than middle-aged teachers (Allensworth et al., 2009), and also that teachers with higher student test score gains are more likely to remain on the staff (Boyd et al., 2011). Other evidence suggests that teachers that have autonomy to teach and that have influence in the school's decision-making process are far more likely to stay in the school. Such research knowledge should at least give us a focal point for initiating a turnover reduction plan.

Working conditions also influence teacher attrition. Along with the previously mentioned factors of principal support and teaching autonomy, many other factors serve to condition school climate. The topic of school climate is discussed in depth in Chapter 4.

Increasing Teacher Retention: Your Leadership Looms Important

One lesson learned concerning teacher retention rests in the fact that administrative support is a crucial factor in teachers' decisions to remain or leave their teaching position. The problem is vested in the need to know what support is most instrumental as a positive influence for retention. Support can be viewed from several perspectives. For one individual, for example, support might be viewed as the assistance that a teacher receives relative to instructional improvement, or the mentoring that a teacher receives relative to career aspirations. Another teacher might view administrative support as being given autonomy in his or her classroom teaching and or opportunities to be involved in the important decisions relative to work assignments.

Previous discussions have implied that we really do not have the answers to best practices for teacher retention. Some strategies have been recommended that have been effective for administrators in their situations. We submit that the principal needs to give serious thought to a retention plan that will serve as a guide for positive teacher retention. Like any other plan, a retention guide can serve to help you focus on the important problem of staff stability, can provide your leadership in implementing the plan, and can result in hard evidence for assessing the efficacy of the plan.

Guidelines for Reducing the Loss of Quality Personnel

The following guidelines are recommended:

1. Check the status of staff attrition in your school. Reducing the incidence of staff loss will serve the purpose of knowing who is leaving the school. Is it the teachers new to the school? Is the loss due to teacher retirements? Is it marginal teachers that have found the teaching profession an unsatisfactory pursuit? What age group is leaving? Is it your most talented teachers that are leaving the school? The answers to these questions serve the primary purpose of setting procedures for your retention plan. Figure 2.3 is an example of an exit-interview form that should be administered to every employee that leaves your school on a voluntary basis. An exit-interview report will provide important information as to the reasons employees are leaving, and will often point to the need for administration changes on your part. The report can be completed by using a face-to-face interview, or by having the individual complete the form in writing.

Name (Optional) Date

1. Please tell about your reasons for leaving the school. Know that this information is considered as personal and private and will be used by me as school principal for the purpose of examining our administrative programs and procedures.

2. Were there specific policies and/or administrative procedures that you think were troublesome for you as an employee in the school? If so, do you have suggestions or recommendations for changing them?

3. How would you rate the climate or health of the school's environment on a scale of 1–low to 5–high? Please explain your rating regarding the climate characteristics that were especially positive or negative in your view.

4. Did you take advantage of the various professional growth and development opportunities that were provided by the school or school district? And, how would you rate these opportunities as being beneficial to you on a scale of 1–little value, 2–some value, 3–high value? Please explain. What improvements in the professional development programs might you recommend?

5. Do you plan to remain in teaching? And, if so, will you be teaching in a school district within the state? If not, will you be working in a position outside of education? Please explain.

Thank you,
School Principal

FIGURE 2.3. Exit-Interview Report

2. Design a staff reduction plan that fits the case. It serves to focus procedures on the teachers identified as most likely to leave your school. Without a plan to guide your administrative actions, your attention to the matter of reduction most likely will be sporadic and ineffective. What is your plan to accomplish? Be specific in stating the desired results. Attention should be directed to solutions that appear most appropriate for the case at hand. For example, if first-year teachers are leaving the school, the need to include the efficacy of instructional assistance is imperative. Or, if teacher loss is due primarily to retirements, a plan for re-recruitment looms important. In some cases, a personal visit with a teacher that is nearing retirement eligibility might be sufficient to encourage them to stay. Some school districts are offering retention bonuses.

We also recommend the implementation of a brief questionnaire that is sent to all personnel toward the end of the first school semester and near

Request: The purpose of this request is to gain information concerning your interests in your school assignments for next semester or for the forthcoming school year. It is not always possible to meet such requests, but please know that each request will be reviewed and given my personal consideration. Sara Herr, Principal

Name: ______ Present teaching assignment: ______

Please check one of the following statements: I do not request any changes in my present teaching or extracurricular assignments (____). Or, I request the following consideration(s) for teaching assignments during the (insert second semester or first semester of next year) (____).

If you requested a change in assignments, please complete the following information.

Change in grade level request as follows: ______

Change of course subject(s) requested as follows: ______

Changes in extracurricular assignments requested as follows: ______

List administrative interests, if any: ______

What teaching certifications do you hold presently? ______

Please insert needed explanations, if any: ______

Principal's Response: ______

______ Principal's Signature

______ Date

FIGURE 2.4. Position Assignment Interest Request

the close of the school year to solicit their suggestions for follow-up assignments. For example, Figure 2.4 illustrates such a questionnaire. Although it might not be possible to honor each teacher's suggestions or requests, the act itself demonstrates your interest in gaining their interest in fostering work satisfaction.

3. Put your plan in action by implementing the strategies suggested. Such strategies include continuous attention to the condition of the school climate, providing opportunities for faculty and support personnel to participate in relevant professional growth activities, attending to the work-life balance of employees, giving positive feedback to individual employees

regarding their contributions to the achievement of school goals and objectives, and implementing personal assistance that serves to bond the employee with the school and its mission.

In regard to retaining talent in the school, you must let talented teachers and support staff know that they are amazing, and that it is obvious that teaching is the career for them; otherwise they could be lost.

4. Attend to the assessments of the effectiveness of the human resource processes that you have in operation. The effectiveness of the processes of recruitment, selection, assignment, orientation and development has great influence on the school's ability to retain stability in the teaching and support staffs.
5. Schedule time to update yourself on the research and best practices pertaining to the human resources function. One of the most important things that you can do to improve your knowledge, skill and confidence in the administration of the human resources function is to assume a research posture. The principal that has a research posture is a student of research, a dispenser of meaningful research results, and a consumer of relevant research in practice. We have reported that studies on teacher retention show that the school principal's support in providing personal assistance to teachers is the most important factor in retaining teachers and staff. Such findings, to be meaningful, must be implemented.

Establishing Safety in the School: How to Deal With Immediate Threats

Safety in the workplace has moved toward the top of the list as a human resources responsibility for school principals. Once again, suggested provisions differ widely for protecting the safety of both students and the school staff. Security measures range from implementing various safety drills for students in classrooms, to permitting teachers to place more security officers on campus, and to placing guns in the hands of teachers. Just how principals should provide protection to students and staff personnel is controversial at best.

The following section focuses on the school principal and immediate threats, rumors of threats and violence that might occur. As noted by the National School Safety and Security Services (1996–2012), "School threat assessment is a gray area and administrators often find themselves walking a tightrope. Nine out of 10 threats may turn out to be unfounded, but no school administrator wants to be number 10." The best information regarding what to do about managing such things as bomb threats or dealing with a disturbed individual that has entered a classroom with a gun in hand, is to have on hand and follow a definite emergency crises plan that has been set forth in advance.

Anticipating emergency events related to threats and violence demands the development of written guidelines to follow in such cases as fires, illegal intruders bursting into a classroom, rumors of a bomb plot, a threat of a gang shooting to take place at the school written on the bathroom wall, or a telephone call to the school office stating that a certain teacher would be hurt within the next two days. Such guidelines provide all those concerned with information regarding procedures for meeting such situations. Such safety guidelines are brief statements relating to a fire in the school, an unwanted entry into a teacher's classroom, a rumor of a violent act such as a bomb threat or intent of performing a personal injury. For each possible occurrence, such as a gun threat by an individual who has entered the school, the guidelines provide information on how to respond, what not to do, whom to call and the number to call, security officers' contact number, and other safety precautions that fit the case. Developing such emergency guidelines and having periodic informational discussions about them with faculty and support personnel, students and parents are important recommendations.

Although it is of paramount importance that the school district has a safety guideline statement in effect, the National School Safety and Security Services (1996–2012) recommends that it is essential that schools should:

1. Treat all threats seriously;
2. Investigate the incident promptly and seriously;
3. Use support staff and external resources as a part of a multidisciplinary threat assessment team to evaluate threats;
4. Take appropriate disciplinary and criminal enforcement steps;
5. Document threats and actions taken; and
6. Enhance security measures, as appropriate, to assure the safety of all students, staff and facilities.

It should be kept in mind that many threats of violence at schools are meant to disrupt education. Closing the school each time a threat is received results in an important loss of academic instruction. Although, as principal, you must deal with the issue, it seems best to do so with a plan to keep the school open and the instructional program in place.

In an effort to deal more directly with school safety measures, most school districts have adopted administrative policies that give some direction as to what must be done in cases of threats or personal harm. An example of such a policy follows:

> In the case of personal threat or immediate harm of self or students, the person or persons involved will immediately take steps to protect students by implementing the protection drills such as duck-and-cover drills or evacuation drills that are practiced monthly. At the very first opportunity, the individual will then notify the school principal and the security officers of the school. The school principal will immediately implement the school's safety procedures by alerting all personnel and security officers of the situation at hand. In turn, the principal will inform the central school district's office of the immediate problem. Together steps will be taken to resolve the problem at hand by protecting the safety of the staff person and students.

Keep in mind that a district board policy is a general statement that sets answers to the question of "what to do" and leaves open the use of discretion by the administration to establish regulations for implementing the policy. Thus, specific school procedures, including emergency guidelines, can be established for each school as fits the case.

How the School Principal Establishes Fairness in the Workplace

Besides protection from physical violence and threats from disturbed persons, the HR safety and protection responsibilities of the school principal include many other factors. Legal rights for teachers, such as due process and other issues including job security, academic freedom, employee grievances and unfair treatment, are causes of many court litigations. For students, student rights, student protection and student suspension are directly in the hands of the school principal. Chapter 5 of this book deals specifically with the legal world of the school principal in relation to the aforementioned provisions.

Summary

Establishing a solid foundation for the implementation of the HR processes through an effective planning process was a major theme of this chapter. Ineffective planning activities will be certain to result in inferior HR outcomes. The concept of completing position analyses with follow-up position descriptions at the local school level will come as a new responsibility for most school principals. Nevertheless, the time and effort spent doing so will substantially reduce the time that the principal will have to spend in implementing the HR processes of recruitment, selection, orientation, development and others.

It has been said that one of the worst things that a school principal can do is to make a bad hire. The chapter's recommendations for implementing the processes of recruitment and selection will serve to reduce the hiring of unqualified personnel.

The growing concept of a balanced work-life has moved slowly into the profession of education. Improving job satisfaction through such provisions as flexible work schedules is one of the concepts that indeed are finding their way into practice at the local school level.

The importance of the safety of personnel has been demonstrated by the tragic events that have occurred nationally in schools today. The factor of bringing about equitable teaching assignments has yet to be resolved. Inequities in the workloads of teachers continue, and, as a result, the performance of many quality teachers has been reduced to a level of actual mediocrity. Equitable load assignments can be realized, and tools such as the Douglass Teacher Load Formula can serve the school principal well.

One of the important challenges facing school principals today is that of retaining a viable workforce. The factors that can contribute to the retaining of talented personnel were presented in this chapter. The subjects of job satisfaction and school climate are discussed in Chapters 3 and 4.

Discussion Questions

1. **Group Discussion**. Divide the members of the class into small groups. Each group is asked to give examples of effective planning in their schools or in a school with which they are most familiar. Have each group report back on the nature of their planning experiences and the effectiveness of these activities as they have experienced them.
2. Review the section that focused on the development of a position analysis. Study the contents that are commonly included in a position analysis. Then, give thought to the development of a position analysis for your current education assignment. Would such a tool have been of value to you as you entered your present assignment as a teacher, assistant principal, principal or other position in education?
3. A challenge. Review the section in the chapter on measuring teacher load. Then calculate the teacher load of a teacher who has the following load

factors. If you get really serious and want more information, check the teacher load references at the end of this chapter (the Douglass and Norton/Bria formulas are discussed in Norton, 2008).

- Teacher C teaches 3 classes of American history with 22, 25, and 29 students each day (five times each week). Grades 11 and 12.
- Teacher C teaches 2 classes of Government. Grade 12.
- Class periods are 50 minutes in length.
- No classes in the assignment are duplicates.
- The teacher averages 500 per semester on cooperative duties (equal to 10 class periods).

The SGC (subject grade coefficient) of American history and government is 1.0.

The Douglass Teacher Load Formula:

$$SGC = \left(CP - \frac{DUP}{10} + \frac{NP - 25CP}{100}\right)\left(\frac{PL + 50}{100}\right) + .6\ PC\left(\frac{PL + 50}{100}\right)$$

TL = ________ ?

Abbreviation Key:

CP — Class periods per week
DUP — Duplications per week
NP — Number of pupils in classes per week
PL — Period length in minutes (class periods)
PC — Periods of cooperative duties
TL — Total load index

Case Studies

Case 2.1. Say, Sara, I Have a Great Teacher Candidate for You!

Angelo Martinez, school board member for the Waverly School District, sent an email message to Sara Ortiz indicating that he had a great candidate for the 4th-grade opening at the Waverly school. Mr. Martinez stated that he knew the parents of Mary Manuel very well, and had met Miss Manuel at a recent neighborhood picnic. She was quite friendly and had taught previously in a neighboring school district. She had left her teaching position to become a sales representative for a local business firm, but now had hopes of reentering the teaching profession.

Principal Ortiz replied by email to the board member saying thanks, and indicating that she would ask for Ms. Manuel's credentials. Principal Ortiz examined the credentials of Mary Manuel and also presented them at the next meeting of the school's search committee. In addition, she called the neighboring school principal where Mary had taught previously.

The feedback given by the school's search committee and by the principal in the neighboring school district, along with the references in Mary's credentials were not altogether positive. Principal Ortiz was in agreement.

Within the next two weeks, board member Martinez called Principal Ortiz and asked how the Mary Manuel thing was going. As diplomatically as possible, Principal Ortiz told him that Mary Manuel did not have the qualities that were hoped for in a teacher at Waverly Elementary.

There was a short silence before board member Martinez said, "Well, I suggest that you reconsider this matter once again. You know the difficulty that we have recruiting teachers for our school district. I don't see how we can pass on Mary Manuel."

Question:

Assume the role of Principal Ortiz. On the basis of the information given in Case Study 2.1, do you think that you did the right thing? Are you going to consider the matter further? If so, what do you plan to do? Be prepared to make a follow-up call to Mr. Martinez after informing the director of human resources and perhaps the school superintendent relative to your position on this matter.

References

Allensworth, E., Ponisciak, S., & Mazzeo, C. (2009). *The schools teachers leave: Teacher mobility in Chicago public schools.* Chicago, IL: Consortium on Chicago School Research at the University of Chicago Urban Education Institute.

Alliance for Excellent Education. (2008). Missouri State. Retrieved from http://www.all4ed.org/about_the_crisis/schools/state_information/missouri

Baird, L., Meshoulam, L., & DeGive, G. (1983). Meshing human resources planning with strategic planning: A model approach. *Personnel, 60*(5), 14–25.

Bathhurst, P. (2007, March 11). Training is the key at top firms. *Arizona Republic*, p. ED1.

Berglas, W. W. (1973). A study of relationships between induction practices and the morale of the beginning teacher. *Dissertation Abstracts International, 34*(5), 2189–A.

Boyd, D., Grossman, P., Ing, M., Lankford, H., Loeb, S., & Wyckoff, J. (2011). The influence of school administrators on teacher retention decisions. *American Educational Research Journal, 48*(2), 303–333.

Goetz, B. E. (1949). *Management planning and control.* New York, NY: McGraw-Hill.

Goodstein, L. D., Pfeiffer, J. W., & Nolan, T. M. (1986). *Applied strategic planning: A comprehensive guide.* New York, NY: McGraw-Hill.

Hanlon, J. M. (1968). *Administration and education.* Belmont, CA: Wadsworth.

Harris, D. N., Rutledge, S. A., Ingle, W. K., & Thompson, C. C. (2010). Mix and match: What principals look for when hiring teachers. *Education Finance and Policy, 5*(2), 228–246.

Heathfield, S. M. (2013). Ten top human resources trends of the decade. Retrieved from http://humanresources.about.com/of/businessmanagement/a/top_trends.htm

Kowalski, T. J., McDaniel, P., Place, A. W., & Reitzug, U. C. (1992). Factors that principals consider most important in selecting new teachers. *ERS Spectrum, 10*(3), 34–38. National School Safety and Security Services. (1996–2012). *School threats, school violence rumors and school threat assessment.* Retrieved from http://www.schoolsecurity.org/trends/threat-assessment-threats-rumors-text-messages/

Norton, M. S. (2008). *Human resources administration for educational leaders.* Thousand Oaks, CA: Sage.

Peterson, L. J., Rossmiller, R. A, & Volz, M. M. (1978). *The law and public school operation* (2nd ed.). New York, NY: Harper & Row.

Salpeter, J. (2003, August 15). Professional development: 21st century models. *Tech and Learning.* Retrieved from http://www.techlearning.com/features/0039/professional-development-21st–century-models/45151

SHRM (Society for Human Resource Management). (2012, November 1). Challenges facing HR over the next 10 years. Retrieved from http://www.shrm.org/Research/Survey Findings/Articles/Pages/ChallengesFacingHROvertheNext10Years.aspx

Young, I. P. (2008). *The human resource function in educational administration* (9th ed.). Upper Saddle River, NJ: Pearson, Merrill/Prentice Hall.

CHAPTER

3 Providing for Personal and Professional Growth and Development for All School Personnel

Primary chapter goal:

To extend the foundational concept that schools are people, and to emphasize the vital importance of the principal's leadership in implementing a planned program of personal growth and development for school effectiveness and success.

One of the foundational themes of this book is that organizations will progress as the people in them grow and develop. The concept that school principals must be human resources leaders includes the fact that they must be staff development leaders as well. Empirical evidence in business and industry reveals that one of the most important factors for fostering job satisfaction is providing opportunities for employees to increase their knowledge and skill levels toward the goal of career development.

Staff Development: Your School Will Progress as Personnel Grow and Develop

Staff development should be viewed as a self-development process that centers on the personal interests and needs of the individual employee as well as the needs of the school. An important fact to remember is that effective staff development is not a single event but a human resources process. One thing is certain: the school principal's leadership skill in providing continuous opportunities for the growth and development of each member of the faculty and classified staff will go far in determining the effectiveness of the school's ultimate success.

We encourage school leaders to avoid reactive provisions when implementing staff development activities. Reactive development is programmed exclusively by the administrative staff according to its thinking of what the staff needs to meet program needs. Every employee receives the same program. Such an approach commonly is accepted with apathy, whereby the employee comes to the required in-service session, sits down, and says to himself or herself, "OK, grow me!" We believe that such an approach is ineffective and its outcomes are short-lived. A proactive strategy does consider organizational needs, but the personal and professional needs of the employee are given first consideration. It focuses on extending the personal interests and strengths of the teacher, as opposed to spending the majority of time on the remediation of identified weaknesses.

Growth is personal in the sense that what motivates each individual is a personal matter and each person's self-image is instrumental in determining what incentives will encourage personal growth. Staff development is self-development in that growth begins with a personal need, and individuals develop by being willing to take responsibility for their own professional growth. This concept does not mean that personal development is not to be enhanced through the support of others, but that personal growth is mainly an intrinsic rather than extrinsic phenomenon (Norton, 2008, p. 196).

Staff Development: Implementing the Right Program at the Right Time

Practicing school principals are quick to point out that timing is key for "selling" a staff development program or activity. For example, as one principal noted, "heavy lifting" staff development activities commonly are not effective if scheduled just before holidays. After-school scheduling also presents obvious inhibitors to successful development activities. Teachers have been engaged in arduous teaching activities for several hours and adding more hours after school for staff development is problematic.

How to Foster a Learning Atmosphere in the School Through Staff Development

Empirical evidence gathered through interviews with practicing school principals, examining research on the topic of staff development, and observing staff development programs in schools has led to several conclusions that are presented in the next section. In some cases, the conclusion focuses on a consensus of research findings; in others it represents agreements on best practices from staff development experiences of many school leaders and also the results of personal experience. Not every conclusion or recommendation is possible or workable in every other school. Nevertheless, the ideas that follow will conjure up tips for use in your school situation, or suggest other related staff development activities that you could implement tomorrow.

Staff Development Is a Human Resources Process

As previously noted, effective staff development is not a single event; rather, it is an ongoing and planned human resources process. This concept infers that staff development, just like any other HR process, requires serious planning that ties closely to the mission of the school and the primary objective of achieving improved student achievement. So when individual teachers or organized staff development teams initiate staff development activities, they begin by assessing their needs and interests, in terms of what performance improvements are needed in order to close the gaps between current practices and student learning results. Thus, the intent of staff development activities is to focus on making meaningful connections between growth experiences and learning outcomes. In short, activities and programs of staff development should center on the goals and objectives of the school's curricular program and address the new knowledge needed to bridge the gaps that have been diagnosed between the desired goals and objectives and the current program results.

The School Principal Opens the Door for Staff Development Opportunities

The following section describes several staff development activities commonly used by school principals in practice. Staff development is a cooperative activity that often involves personnel in the central district office, various professional personnel within the community, teachers on the school staff and educational professors from colleges and universities. The principal's development activities related to the performance appraisal are detailed in a later section of the chapter.

Staff Development Is Self-Development

In the end, the effectiveness of staff development programs depends in large part on the initiative, motivation and attitude of the individual staff member. It isn't that other persons and/or offices in the school are not important in supporting and providing significant staff development assistance, or that staff development teaming is not beneficial, but the staff development experience most likely will be taken lightly unless the individual staff member has been directly involved in deciding its purposes, provisions and learning methods. Only through such involvement will the staff member be able to take up a feeling of personal ownership for the staff development activities, and be able to assume a personal accountability for its success.

Following the staff development activity and having an opportunity to implement the new knowledge and skills required in classroom instruction, the individual makes his or her own personal assessment of the true benefits of the experience. Such success tends to foster a sense of commitment to the continued use of the development's results, and fosters an attitude that encourages continuous personal growth.

Staff Development Requires Time and Support Resources

The barometer that shows what is being stressed and where instructional time is being spent is a good clue to showing what is viewed as important in the minds of school leaders and their staffs. The concept of administrative support for staff development carries with it the need to provide time for it. Building team collaboration and cooperation necessitates the arranging of released time for individual staff members to participate and staff development team members to meet and confer. Staff development activities such as workshops, mentoring, practicing, peer teaching and observing, participating and demonstrating require scheduled time on the part of both staff development presenters and those participants that are involved in the learning process.

Can you envision the implementation of a classroom visitation and a follow-up performance appraisal report all completed through means of technology? The video camera tapes and records both the visual and audio aspects of the classroom visitation, which can then aid in assessing the performance relative to the predetermined traits commonly expected in a quality teaching performance. Impossible? We discuss the topic of performance appraisal in the next major section of the chapter.

A Look at a Few Successful Practices

Here are a few ways in which some schools have provided staff development time for staff members:

1. Arrange extended time for planning and implementation of the plan by organizing such programs as scientists-for-teacher days, when qualified community persons in related science work assume the role of teachers for a day while school staff development teams meet or attend professional growth activities.
2. Arrange for quality large-group instruction whereby students attend presentations in the auditorium that are presented by celebrities from a variety of fields while teachers are released to participate in planned staff development activities.
3. Get approval to dismiss students one day each month while individual teachers and staff development teams do their thing in regard to development plans.
4. Some school districts have utilized weekends and certain days for staff development purposes. When this arrangement is implemented, empirical evidence indicates that it is the teachers' groups that have recommended it. One school district awarded participants by giving them credits toward an upgrade on the teachers' salary schedule. One principal reported that new teachers to the school were given one less class to teach during their first year so that the orientation process could be more effective, and time for initial staff development activities could be assured.
5. Schools that report successful staff development programs, in almost all cases, have had financial support in the school's budget. Such funding commonly is contingent on the basis that the staff development activity or program has been developed cooperatively by the teaching staff and school principal, and, in some cases, the central office director of human resources must approve the development activity as well.

A description or discussion of all of the possible staff development options available to schools is much beyond the scope of this section. Each time that we visit with school principals about their staff development successes, some new and intriguing activity commonly comes to mind. We call this a "light bulb experience." On many occasions, it does not take attendance at a professional conference or a two-hour workshop to spark a new idea for one's consideration. A "light bulb experience" can happen during a brief conversation with a colleague or during a meeting with a coach or mentor. The following section offers a brief description of some of the common staff development activities being implemented successfully by school staff development principals today.

Principal and Peer Coaching/Mentoring

Most everyone in education has experienced the times that a supervisor or peer has made a brief statement that has come to mind from time to time over the years. "I have always been amazed by your personal initiative," or "The key to reaching your goal of becoming a school principal is just to do what you are doing better than anyone else can do it," or "You are what I view as being a true student advocate." In most cases, you really had not given much thought to the fact that you possessed such positive traits, but the thought has stayed with you and it has become one of your strengths.

Mentoring benefits should not be limited only to teachers or principals new to their roles, but should continue for as long as the mentor and protégé view it as beneficial. The mentor and protégé relationship is a rewarding endeavor that enhances the careers of both the mentor and the protégé. Both learn more about themselves, improve their personal administration skills and gain professional recognition.

Teachers that we have interviewed often mention the fact that one-on-one personal relationships with school leaders and peers are especially beneficial. Coaching and mentoring are such examples and commonly are used interchangeably in education. However, the two terms do have some differences.

Coaching, according to Allegra (Personal communication, 2005) helps a person think through alternative solutions to important career decisions facing them. The focus is on helping the individual to develop career goals by focusing on their personal interests and strengths, and giving them encouragement and support in the achievement of their aspirations.

The **mentoring** activity centers on helping a protégé in the same professional field. Thus, a school principal or peer would be helping a teacher establish networks for developing a plan for continuous professional growth and development, fostering professional growth through providing beneficial feedback and professional support, and offering experience and expertise relative to successful practices in teaching and learning. Neither coaches nor mentors tell their protégés just how they should decide what to do or exactly how to do something. Rather, they serve to help the individual think through their own best solutions and practices that fit the case at hand.

The basic procedure for implementing a mentor and protégé program consists of three primary phases:

1. Establishing the mentor/protégé relationship, including the designing of the individual development plan (IDP) for each protégé;
2. Implementing the IDP;
3. Cultivating a continuing, collegial relationship between the mentor and protégé; and
4. Measuring the success of the plan through various assessments, including self-evaluations administered by the protégé.

The selection of a mentor is one key to the success of the mentoring program. A good principal might not be a good mentor. Mentor qualifications include a number of important traits. The individual:

- has participated in a qualified mentor-training program;
- is recognized as a competent and experienced school administrator;
- is knowledgeable about the responsibilities and problems that commonly face school principals in schools today;
- is knowledgeable about best practices in the administration of school programming, including human resources, instructional leadership, pupil personnel services and other major functions of educational administration;
- understands the social and political aspects and dynamics of administering a school and school system;
- is a good listener;
- has committed himself or herself to the benefits of mentoring for both parties, and has made arrangements in his or her work schedule to carry out the mentoring program effectively.

Capitalizing on Individual Efforts of Growth and Development

We noted previously that staff growth and development in the end is self-development. Growth and development activities that are initiated by individual teachers and support personnel are broad-based and often more successful than structured group programs. As one example, a group of teachers involved in team teaching can divide development activities among members. One teacher might interview teachers at other schools concerning their successful methods for individualizing instruction in the subject area of interest, while another teacher enrolls in a special class on teaching methods in the same subject area. Another teacher might investigate effective material resources available for instructional purposes, and so forth. Whenever a team member is ready, he or she reports back to the entire team so that all members benefit.

In schools where there is a high failure statistic, a department chair or individual teacher could benefit the entire school by examining and collecting the volumes of research that are available on the topic of student retention. Again, reporting a consensus of the research to the school principal and entire faculty would open the eyes of all professional personnel.

While working in Salina, Kansas, a superintendent had the opportunity to ask a neighborhood physician what he did to keep abreast of the rapid changes in the medical field. What did he do relative to professional growth and development? The physician gave his brief answer as follows: "I consider professional growth to be an ongoing responsibility of mine that takes place all the time. I owe it to my patients." Such an attitude fits professional education as well. Educators owe it to their students.

Snapshot 1—Leave Us the Hell Alone, We're Professionals

Dr. Rex Norris was the new director of instruction at the Wymore School District. The position of director of instruction was the first time that Wymore had implemented this role in the school district, although the district did have coordinators of elementary and secondary education in the school district's office. As the new administrator in the district office, he was asked to meet and speak with many community groups and various school faculties. During the teachers' reporting week of his first year as director, he was asked to speak to the Wymore Teachers Association at its first meeting of the year.

Dr. Norris was asked to speak about his new role as director of curriculum. He was introduced to the teachers' assembly and opened his remarks by expressing his pleasure at being selected to the new position in the school district. He went on to talk about looking forward to working with the several schools and their faculties in the area of curriculum development and professional development considerations needed to meet the many changes taking place in education today. Toward the close of his brief comments, Dr. Norris asked if there were questions.

A male teacher in the audience stated, "Just leave us the hell alone, we're professionals!"

The director stood silent for two or three seconds and then commented. "No, you're not. Not if indeed you are a professional. Both empirical evidence and scientific research present evidence indicating that providing opportunities for professional growth and development on the job are ranked near the top of the factors which professionals seek for job satisfaction. Lack of such opportunities is also one of the major factors for the school district's ability to retain quality teachers."

Dr. Norris received his first standing ovation as a member of the Wymore School District.

Note: Think about the situation in Snapshot 1. It represents a true happening, but of course the names of the director and school district are fictitious. The snapshot does present a positive ending, but other results certainly could have happened. Try to put yourself in the shoes of Dr. Norris. What might you have done and/or said in the same situation?

The School Principal: Leading by Example

It has been emphasized throughout this chapter that staff growth and development depends in large part on the leadership of the school principal. School principals who are effective leaders of staff development lead by example. The school staff is quick to see a school leader who is pursuing a planned growth plan himself or herself. One elementary school principal told us that he participates in almost every staff development conference and activity in which teachers partake. He indicated that staff members see him taking notes, and that he holds brief follow-up sessions with staff members to discuss what he has learned. He asks them to report back as well, on questions such as, "What concepts and/or strategies might we pilot in our reading program?" or "Who would like to experiment with the reading for understanding concept emphasized at the conference and report back to all of us your results?"

Staff development leaders are readers, consumers and disseminators of quality research that pertains to the solution of a curriculum problem or learning question faced by the school staff. Many leaders are directly involved in degree programs in their own specialties at institutions of higher learning. They recognize and celebrate occasions when members of the faculty earn a higher degree in their field or are honored for professional contributions that they might have made to their professional association or community. Part of the principal's coaching efforts is reflected in their support of school staff members that are continuing their educational pursuits. Serving as a coach is a demonstration of one's leadership qualities.

Bleedorn (1996) says that leadership should be balanced with followership; that everyone should be given a chance to solo. Personal cooperation and respect for others are the ultimate features in team effectiveness.

What Are the Real Benefits of Performance Appraisals?

According to Hess and Kelly (2005), contrary to popular belief, 80 percent of school principals report that they enjoy a great deal the influence that is associated with the evaluation of teachers. The report did not state whether the enjoyment was relative to formative or summative performance evaluations for teachers. A **summative evaluation** is one in which continuation in the position is the primary concern. A **formative evaluation** focuses on self-improvement of the teacher. The various states and the nation's school districts use different approaches for teacher performance evaluations, but states commonly have passed statutes that regulate the performance evaluation schedules for those persons new to teaching and experienced personnel as well. The facts are that the performance evaluation process takes a great deal of the principal's HR time. The process not only necessitates in-class observations of each teacher's performance, but almost always is followed by a required written report of the evaluation findings and another detailed report of professional growth recommendations that extend from each teacher's evaluation results.

We should make a distinction between the terms "measurement" and "evaluation." **Measurement** is related to the quantified or quasi-quantified description of events, behavior or outcomes, sometimes referred to as **assessments**. **Evaluation** has to do with judgments relating to the quality of behavior and/or results of that behavior in light of objectives agreed upon by the parties involved in the process. The implications are that evaluations must be accompanied by a set of determined objectives. Information must be collected through measurements that require an analysis and interpretation, and through an evaluation that requires judgments on the part of qualified evaluators.

Whether the school principal is the only person who performs teacher evaluations, or whether a team of evaluators participates in teacher evaluations, the need to be a qualified evaluator in most school districts is now a requirement. One way of meeting this requirement is through participation in a qualified evaluator program. Qualified evaluator programs are offered commonly by the school district's HR director and by the state administrators' association or a faculty member of a state college or university. One problem faced by school principals who are implementing the performance evaluation program is the seemingly ongoing changes in the evaluation procedures and requirements. Yet keeping abreast of annual changes in evaluation requirements announced by the state department of education, the school board or a school district office is troublesome, according to the reports of school principals.

Such qualified evaluator programs center on the knowledge and skills needed to appraise a teacher in a classroom setting, and on the procedures for conducting the post-evaluation conference. For example, topics in the area of the classroom observation include the importance of understanding the purposes of the evaluation, learning about the essential components of the evaluation process, understanding the relationships and differences between the supervision and evaluation processes, the methods for identifying and applying the evaluation criteria, and knowing the importance of accurate records concerning the evidence of the criteria in the lesson and achieving inter-rater reliability when more than one evaluator participates.

The major purposes for evaluating personnel are:

1. To identify a basis for improving an employee's performance;
2. To supply information for modification of personnel assignments;
3. To protect individuals or the school (e.g., demonstrate quality performance in meeting program standards);
4. To reward quality performance; and
5. To provide a basis for career planning and individual growth and development.

The volume of literature and reports on the Web relative to the principal's role in teacher evaluations is overwhelming. Articles reporting the procedures for performance appraisal systems set forth by school districts nationally are far more than numerous. One comprehensive example of the teacher performance appraisal system in a Florida county consists of a printed document of 38 pages, perhaps the most comprehensive procedural report that we came across in our study efforts. In addition, new teacher evaluation arrangements between teacher associations, state education officials and state teachers' unions are being debated commonly on a national basis. Much of the debate appears to center on the concept of using student test scores as a large part of the teacher's evaluation score. Another argument is that new evaluation procedures are taking a large portion of a teacher's evaluation out of the hands of the school principal. From a political standpoint, student achievement most likely will continue to be a factor in the final performance score of the teacher.

The point that will be negotiated will be the percentage of test-score results that will be used in the teacher's performance evaluation.

The question is not "Will student test-score results be included in the performance rating of teachers?" but "Should test-score results be included in the performance rating of the teacher?" We take the position that teaching and learning indeed are the primary concerns of education, but that using student test results to determine teacher performance results, especially for salary purposes, is flawed.

Competency-Based Implementation of the HR Performance Evaluation Process

This section focuses on performance evaluation from a competency-based perspective. The primary task of the school principal is to develop the ability to develop and implement an effective plan for evaluating the performance of faculty personnel. The supporting competencies and indicators of competency for the primary task are as follows:

Competency 1. Ability to set school and individual faculty goals regarding the planning and implementation of an effective program for performance evaluation.

Indicators of Competency—Establishes and follows policies and legal procedures for the performance evaluations of professional and support personnel. Understands the differences and purposes between summative and formative activities based on personal interests and needs.

Competency 2. Ability to design/utilize strategies and assessments for determining personnel interests and needs relative to professional growth and development.

Indicators of Competency—Involves staff in the determination of growth activities based on personal interests and needs.

Competency 3. Ability to establish an evaluation program that is in accord with state and local statutes, and one that also meets the policies of the local school district.

Indicators of Competency—Studies and implements an evaluation program that meets the legal requirements of the state and the local school board.

Competency 4. Ability to establish a performance evaluation program that utilizes a variety of performance evaluation strategies, such as self-evaluation instruments, peer evaluation, class observations, performance testing and classroom walk-through evaluations.

Indicators of Competency—Establishes cooperative performance objectives consistent with personal needs and school goals and objectives. Develops and utilizes requirements and definitions of professional competence as the criteria for assessment.

Competency 5. Ability to communicate with individual members of the faculty relative to the performance requirements and personal interests and needs of the employee.

Indicators of Competency—Establishes a rapport with personnel that permits a friendly discussion of personal needs in a mutuality of respect. Gives performance feedback effectively.

Competency 6. Ability to consult with individual members of the faculty and support staff concerning their performance results, and to establish with them specific areas for continued emphasis and those areas that indicate a need for improvement.

Indicators of Competency—Provides guidance for the establishment of an active improvement plan with ongoing reviews of progress. Gives specific support to faculty and staff personnel toward the accomplishment of their individual programs of growth and development by serving as a mentor and coach as fits the case.

Competency 7. Ability to analyze and synthesize evaluation data.

Indicators of Competency—Interprets data in relation to needs for improvement and indications of strength. Develops with appropriate individual(s) professional development programs based on measurements of performance.

Competency 8. Ability to foster job satisfaction and personal pride for faculty and support personnel as appropriate to their contributions to the success of the school's program.

Indicators of Competency—Provides verbal feedback in recognition of personal success toward personal growth and development to members of the school faculty and staff. Makes special efforts to communicate with school personnel, both informally and formally. Demonstrates the concept of "teamness" within the faculty by working cooperatively with individuals, departments and school teams.

Basing Teacher Evaluation Scores on Student Test Results Is on Target—Or Is It?

Basing salary increases on the results of personal performance in the classroom appears to be growing in popularity both in the business and educational worlds. In education, the concept of student testing bases the teacher's salary increase and possible position retention on their students' academic improvement during any one year. But is this an accurate measure of a teacher's effectiveness? We believe that this procedure is an unfair basis for assessing the true effectiveness of a teacher for the following reasons. First of all, research evidence that directly relates test-score results to the classroom performance of a teacher has not been produced. But there are other significant reasons why the practice is troublesome.

Students as individuals mature and learn differently. Cognitive psychology suggests that learning insight among students of the same age occurs in various ways and at different stages of development. Gregorc (2011) points out that sequential learners learn best when learning is structured; they learn best in a linear "building block" manner. On the other hand, abstract learners learn in no particular order. Rather than building-block style, learning for them is more like tinker toys or networking. Ideas, concepts and facts are collected over time, and the student's learning is characterized as being on a plateau.

> Information processing is a cognitive view of learning that compares human thinking to the way computers process information. Information stores—sensory memory, working memory, and long-term memory—hold information; cognitive processes, such as attention, perception, rehearsal, encoding, and retrieval, move the information from one store to another.
>
> (Pearson Education, 1995–2010, p. 1)

A student's former teacher might have had a great contribution to the information stored in the student's network, but insight/achievement as measured by testing might not have taken place during his or her time with the student. If the student's next teacher provides a closing experience that completes connections in the network, a learning spurt occurs. Both teachers should receive credit, but the first teacher's results might not show up on the final test during one year, and the flawed assumption is that he or she did not help the student achieve academically.

Kolb (2011) provides another view of human learning. For example, learners with a divergent style prefer to watch rather than do. Learners with an accommodating style prefer a "hands-on" learning experience. Research supports the fact that some students do not learn effectively from oral instruction. In the same class situation, the auditory learners learn best by listening and speaking. A teacher's teaching style might be contrary to the learning style of some students, but not all of them.

The foregoing facts are only a small part of the complex consideration of how and why some students learn and why some students do not show achievement on tests under one teacher but do show up on achievement tests with another teacher. For example, a student might not master long division in grade 3, but might gather information related to other arithmetical operations that result in his or her ability to master long division later in grade 4.

Contemporary teacher accountability seems to place primary emphasis on student academic achievement in reading, math, English and science. But what about contributions to other important student learning goals such as moral values, self-realization, worthy home membership, salable skills, rational thinking, good health and others? Performance-based salary allocations commonly are overlooked in regard to a teacher's contributions to these goals of paramount importance.

School principal human resources leaders need to step up and inform all those concerned that students do indeed differ, and information relative to how each student learns is no exception. True learning leaders help teachers understand that it is necessary to determine each student's success level in an attempt to find out the learning program for them. That concept serves the purpose of individualizing instruction in the best interests of each student. But basing a teacher's performance evaluation on testing when a teacher's learning contributions have been positive but often do not result in immediate insight is an unfair practice.

Race to the Top Program: Implications for the Teacher Appraisal Process

The U.S. Government's Race to the Top program (R2T) was created as part of the American Recovery and Reinvestment Act of 2009 for the purpose of promoting innovation and reforms in the nation's state and local K–12 school districts. According to Wikipedia (2013), $3,425,000 had been awarded to eleven states and the District of Columbia for the intended purposes of the act. Although the act holds implications for practices in many of the HR processes, it is the purpose here to point out the implications of the act for school districts nationally relative to performance appraisal requirements. For example, in order to be eligible for monetary rewards, school districts had to use value-added modeling in teacher evaluations (Wikipedia, 2013). According to reports, some states changed their performance evaluation laws for education to include this procedure. In brief, value-added procedures necessitate the presentation of hard data showing that the implementation of the program procedures resulted in specific program improvements relative to the act's set of common achievement standards.

School districts, politicians, educators and others criticized the act, indicating that it focused on the use of student testing to evaluate teacher performance. Numerous other criticisms were aimed at the act, including the fact that such reforms had been tried and had failed before, that the competitive aspects of receiving a reward were biased and unfairly distributed, and that the performance standards differed from those currently used by the state.

A Synthesis Model for Planning and Implementing an Effective Teacher Appraisal Performance Program

We need to keep in mind that teacher performance appraisal must serve two primary purposes. First, the informative evaluation serves primarily as the basis for determining and implementing professional growth and development interests and needs relative to classroom instruction. The second summary performance evaluation most often encompasses more than just classroom instruction; rather, it looks at all the important traits of the teacher that result in serving as a quality teacher.

Figure 3.1 illustrates the steps and provisions commonly associated with formative performance appraisals. The model is general in nature, and specific procedures related to each level of operation depend on the state laws, the state department of education's policies, the school district's board of education policies, and the local school district's administrative regulations.

How Important Is the Performance Review?

A great deal of concern is expressed by school personnel relative to the lack of feedback received on their work performance. As previously mentioned, some employees state that they never know just how they stand as a member of the school faculty. Quality personnel need to receive feedback as well as those employees that need to know what they can do to improve their teaching performance. Positive feedback is of paramount importance for fostering personal motivation and job satisfaction. The term "support" commonly

Plan a Teacher Evaluation Program

- Establish initial evaluation program objectives in assessments and evaluations.
- Establish procedures for implementing the evaluation program.
- Clarify personnel assignments and responsibilities.

Implement the Evaluation Program and Maintain System of Evaluation

- Initiate the evaluation activities of pre-observation, classroom visitations, post-conference, and follow-up improvement activities.
- Complete required reports related to assessments, classroom measurements, personal behaviors, and related professional activities.
- Maintain record system according to state statutes and local school district policies and regulations.

Evaluate Effectiveness of the Assessment and Evaluation Programs

- Determine and analyze improvements in individual and group student achievement gains as required by state statutes and local school district policies and regulations.
- Determine gaps between stated goals and objectives and evaluation results.
- Conduct a climate survey that includes teachers, support staff, students and parents regarding the health of the school climate and the positive and/or negative outcomes of the assessment and evaluation process.

FIGURE 3.1. Teacher Performance Appraisal Model

centers on what the school leader is doing to provide assistance to the teacher for helping him or her become a better teacher; that is just what the teacher wants to do.

Positive or improvement feedback can be given to the faculty or staff member at any time. Just a word of appreciation or a suggestion for improvement can be effective for supporting performance behaviors of personnel. However, a planned performance review session is appropriate after a formative or summative performance evaluation is administered.

Before participating in a performance review session, remember what you most likely learned in Educational Administration 101: "Effective leaders are good listeners." You do not have to dominate the discussion. Just giving them something to say at the outset of the session is not sufficient; rather, the teacher should feel comfortable in being an important part of the discussion from start to finish. What does the teacher think is important in this session, and what do they hope would come of it? The teacher's answers open the door for what is important to them, and in most cases, their thoughts lend opportunities for you to discuss your agenda.

It is important to be as diplomatic as possible in dealing with problem areas, but specificity is an absolute as well. Dancing around the problem leaves the teacher in a quandary as to what you are trying to convey. In some cases the individual might wonder if you are talking about them or just presenting a case that does not apply to them. For example, assume that your comment in the session was, "we are having problems in gaining the support of our parents relative to their involvement in their child's education." Whose problem? Your problem? The teacher's problem? What you really want to make clear is that the teacher in the feedback session is not fostering the positive behaviors toward parents that he or she needs to demonstrate. Give examples of evidence that has been collected and ones that the teacher understands are behaviors that he or she has demonstrated in a negative way. Then ask follow-up questions regarding what will be done now to remedy this outcome. Make it clear that this aspect of the teacher's performance must be improved. The problem related to parental support most likely is not the only area of improvement needs on the part of the teacher. Each area must be addressed. There are several ways of extending the performance review and its improvement needs. Ask the teacher to give immediate thought to the areas of needed improvement and submit a statement that focuses on actions to be taken. As principal, review the teacher's plan and submit your feedback on the plan to the teacher in person. All of this activity takes your time; it just might be the best use of your time in the long run.

The Principal and Performance Evaluation of the Support Staff

Empirical evidence suggests that school principals are minimally involved in the recruitment, selection, and professional development of classified personnel. Yet, the responsibility for the performance appraisal of this group of employees often falls to the office of the school principal, since these employees work daily in the local school's environment. Procedures for evaluating the performance of classified personnel follow closely the procedures for all other employees. The school principal commonly meets with the individual or work classes of the classified personnel and explains the appraisal process. Copies of the evaluation instrument are distributed to the employees. The appraisal instrument generally includes a number of performance factors, including job knowledge, quality of work, personal behaviors such as responsibility and dependability, personal relationships, completion of job goals and objectives, and others.

In addition, the personal job improvement targets from previous formative evaluations are included for each individual worker. One section on the appraisal form includes information relative to performance improvement recommendations. Post-evaluation meetings with the employee center on the designing and implementation of the personal growth and development plan for the respective worker.

Figure 3.2 is an excerpt of the Classified Annual Appraisal document used by the Tempe Elementary School District in Arizona. For purposes of illustration, the appraisal excerpt includes only three of the nine performance

Standard 1: Actions and Behaviors

Work Attitude	Always/Almost always exhibits a positive & professional work attitude	Constantly exhibits a positive & professional work attitude	Has difficulty demonstrating a positive & professional work attitude	Rarely demonstrates a positive & professional work attitude

Standard 2: Knowledge and Organization of Work

Knowledge of Work	Always/Almost always demonstrates a mastery of job knowledge, completing work accurately	Constantly performs work accurately & completely	Has difficulty completing work accurately	Rarely completes work accurately

Standard 3: Employee, Student and Public Relations

Employee, Student, & Public Relations	Always/Almost always a positive role model & promotes the District in a positive manner	Constantly promotes a positive atmosphere	Has difficulty promoting a positive atmosphere	Rarely interacts with others in a manner that creates a positive atmosphere

Professional Growth Plan

Strategies to Achieve Objectives

Overall Rating

Overall Score: __Exemplary __Proficient __Needs Improvement __Does Not Meet Standards

Employee Signature ______________________ Date: __________
Evaluator Signature ______________________ Date: __________

FIGURE 3.2. Classified Staff Member Annual Appraisal—An Excerpt

standards on the original assessment appraisal form, but also includes a section for a professional growth plan that is mutually determined by the support staff member and the school principal. Other assessment standards include the performance factors of initiative, compliance with rules and regulations, personal appearance and others. A school could insert other assessment standards that fit its situation.

Summary

The effectiveness of the principal's planning activities will influence each of the major HR processes that are administered in the school. Unless a solid foundation is established that sets forth purposes and objectives for recruitment, selection, assignment and other HR processes, guidelines for determining "what to do" and "how it is to be accomplished" will result in sporadic decisions and chaos.

The extent to which the HR function has been delegated to the local school does vary within the states and among school districts. But it is clear in contemporary practice that the school principal is now involved in every HR process within the HR function. Even the salary process has found its way to the principal's office. Special federal programs relating to teacher improvement have necessitated monetary distributions to teachers on a competitive basis.

Quality teacher requirements have necessitated new looks at traditional recruitment and selection processes. Position analysis and the development of comprehensive position descriptions are now essential, both for legal reasons and for definitive work assignments. The qualified teacher is viewed in a different light in federal and state statutes, and this has resulted in making the process of teacher evaluation an ongoing, everyday responsibility for practicing principals.

The orientation and assignment processes have increased in importance, due primarily to their relationship to both voluntary and involuntary staff retention. Inequities in teacher loads have necessitated a more scientific approach to measuring the workload of teachers and to the matter of retaining teacher talent.

The concept that schools will progress as the people in them grow and develop was emphasized in this chapter. Staff development was viewed as a self-development activity; effective development centers on the interests and needs of the school personnel. The school principal leads in providing a variety of growth and development opportunities for both the professional and support staff.

Discussion Questions

1. Planning in regard to the administration of the HR function at the local school level was emphasized in the chapter as being of high importance. Give some thought to the HR process of planning as it occurs in your school or in a school with which you are familiar. To what extent do you believe that effective HR planning is taking place at the local school level? Do not be satisfied with a simple answer of "being well done" or "being poorly done," but set forth specific evidence that supports your response. (Note: If this exercise is done in a class situation, have individuals or small groups present their responses and then take some time to review the importance of the HR planning process.)
2. Differentiate between formative and summative performance evaluations in regard to their purposes and follow-up activities. Then consider the following question: Should the same qualified evaluator be the individual that does both the formative and summative performance evaluations for the same employee? Why or why not?
3. Give some thought to the ongoing professional growth and development process that is practiced in schools today. In most situations, every teacher must be a quality teacher as defined by statutes. What performance measurements and evaluations are being required by state and federal agencies today?
4. Take time to review the chapter's information regarding recommendations for implementing effective professional development programs, and give an informed opinion as to the quality of the local school development program with which you are most familiar. What is its rating on a scale of 1 (low) to 10 (high)? If the rating is 6 or below, what needs to be done to improve the program?
5. Should the school principal be given the responsibility for serving as the qualified evaluator for support staff personnel (e.g., secretarial staff, maintenance staff, cafeteria staff, security personnel and teacher aides)? Why or why not? Support your response with specific rationale and evidence.

Case Studies

Case 3.1. Why Can't We Retain Our Support Personnel?

Donn White, principal of Southeast High School, sat back in his office chair and wondered why he was facing the problem again of retaining classified staff personnel. He knew that competition for several of the classified job families was making it difficult to attract quality secretaries and maintenance workers, but now losses of personnel in the food service area had become troublesome, along with the fact that two security officers had resigned during the first semester.

He decided to schedule a meeting with the director, Bud Folsom, with the hope that he could find some way of attacking the problem.

"Come in, Donn," said director Folsom. "Like you, I have been concerned with the personnel turnover at Southeast for some time. Frankly, I don't understand it. Our salary situation is competitive among other school districts and above the districts of Lafayette and Washington, and they are closest to our location."

"Yes, I know," answered Donn. "I had exit interviews with most of the employees who left the school last year. I could not determine just why they were leaving, but a couple of them left to join private companies."

"I have read several studies of worker job satisfaction and they all contend that salary isn't the primary cause of poor morale," said director Folsom. "The studies seem to imply that factors such as supervisor relationships and working conditions are those that lead to job dissatisfaction. Donn, you're closer to the situation at your school than I am, let's hear what steps you recommend at this time."

Discussion:

If in a group situation, have each group assume the role of principal Donn White. Put the best thoughts of group members together and develop a follow-up plan to recommend to director Folsom. Avoid suggesting overly general recommendations such as forming a committee to study the matter. Set forth a brief, specific plan that can be implemented immediately that carries with it an accountability procedure for assessing its success.

If acting alone, follow the same procedure as above and set forth the plan that you would recommend.

Case 3.2. We Need a Professional Growth and Development Plan That Works!

The Whittier School District's elementary, middle school and secondary school coordinators of curriculum cooperated in implementing the district's personnel growth and development programs for the 425 school teachers in the school district. The school board's policy on professional growth stipulated that a qualified teacher-training program was to be implemented each year, and that 10 professional growth credits would be awarded for each 8-hour growth program attended. Although attendance at the growth and development programs was voluntary, a teacher's performance plan often recommended one or more of the development programs for teachers with performance deficiencies.

The school board's growth and development policy also called for an annual report of the program services at least one time each year. At a recent school board meeting, the three district curriculum coordinators reported on the program. Between the months of August and March, eight growth and development programs had been scheduled; each program consisted of four 2-hour class sessions. Each program utilized one or more experts on such topics as school safety procedures, parental involvement in the school, bullying, the district testing program, cafeteria management and school menus, team teaching and implications of the state's educational bills pending in the legislature. The honorariums for the eight experts totaled $4,800 plus any travel expenses. The eight development programs had been attended by a total of 110 teachers, although 20 teachers had attended two of the eight programs.

One board member commented that attendance figures appeared to reveal that approximately 25 percent of the professional staff had attended the eight development sessions.

In reply, the high school curriculum coordinator pointed out that several teachers in the school system were working on advanced degree programs, primarily at the master's degree level. Then, too, the after-program survey showed that a high percentage of the attendees, 72 percent, indicated that they enjoyed the development program sessions.

The school board president thanked the district coordinators for their report. Another board member asked if a motion might be in order at this time or during the business session to follow. He indicated that he wanted to move that the matter of the growth and development program be scheduled again for discussion at the board work session that was to take place in two weeks.

Questions:

1. Read carefully once again the foregoing case information. What comments and/or points seem to come to mind as you think about the board report?
2. What do you think that the board member had in mind when he asked that the matter of the professional growth and development program be discussed at the board work session next week?
3. Assume that you are a school principal in the Whittier School District. Assume also that you were invited by the school board president to attend the next school board work session. What preparation might you think about and/or make prior to the work session, if any?

Case 3.3. Support Staff Members' Concern About Performance Pay

MEMO

To: Carl Hulbert, Principal, Wymore High School

From: Pat Ramirez and Bobbie Evans, Co-Chairs, Wymore High School Support Staff

Re: Classified Employees' Concern Regarding Performance Pay Movement

Date: March 14

As you know, we serve as the school's co-chairs of the Wymore High School Support Staff. We want to express our concern about what we believe is a detrimental move for Wymore Classified Personnel. That is, we have heard that talks have been taking place on performance-based pay for classified personnel. Although our group at Wymore High has not received any report of official action on this matter to date, we have yet to be brought into the picture for our views on this matter.

We believe that immediate action should be taken on this matter since the concern is increasing daily. As you know, performance pay for classified personnel has not been well received in other school districts and likely would not work here as well.

Since your opinion would weigh heavily on any decision about performance-based pay for our high school, we would like to know just how you stand on this issue. What are your views on the matter of performance-based pay? Are you about to support such a movement for our school, and if so, why?

Since our school's classified employees meet in early April, we hope to be able to report your response to the group at our next meeting. Please know that we understand that you do not make final decisions on salary matters such as the one of our concern. However, you are in a leadership position and represent us as part of the Wymore High School team.

Pat Ramirez, Cafeteria Manager, and Bobbie Evans, Journey Plumber, Wymore High School

cc: Violet Smith, President, Wymore Classified Personnel Assn.

Question:

Assume the role of Principal Hulbert and set forth your response to the classified personnel members at your school. Avoid sidestepping the response by indicating that such matters are not within your jurisdiction. Set forth your stand on the matter at hand, including the reasons for the position that you assume.

References

Bleedorn, B. D. (1996, November 11). For lesson in teamwork, try listening to some jazz. *Star Tribune* (Minneapolis, MN). *Monday Business*, Business Forum, Commentary.

Gregorc, A. (2011). *Mind styles.* Retrieved from http://web.cortland.edu/andersmd/learning/Gregorc.htm

Hess, F. M., & Kelly, A. P. (2005). The accidental principal. *Education Next, 5*(3), 3441.

Kolb, D. (2011). Kolb learning styles. Retrieved from http://www.businessballsco/kolb learningstyles.htm

Norton, M. S. (2008). *Human resources administration for educational leaders.* Thousand Oaks, CA: Sage.

Pearson Education. (1995–2010). Chapter 7: Cognitive views of learning [Chapter outline and summary]. Retrieved from http://wps.prenhall.com/chet_eggen_education_6/0,8057,885470-,00.html

Wikipedia. (2013, November 5). Race to the top. Retrieved from http://en.wikipedia.org/wii/Race-to_the_Top#Criticisms

CHAPTER

4

School Climate: A School Principal's Magic Wand

Primary chapter goal:

To underscore the vital importance of fostering a positive school climate in the school for meeting the primary goals and objectives of the school's mission.

A Two-Minute Quiz

We ask that you take the following two-minute quiz that provides some feedback concerning your thinking relative to the topic of this chapter; that of school climate. Your score on the quiz could allow you to skip the information in this chapter. On the other hand, it is quite possible that the quiz itself will be beneficial for you to examine the status of school climate practices in schools and other organizations today.

The Quiz

Directions: For each of the ten statements, answer True or False. Do not merely guess if you do not know the answer. You are the only one that will see your score, so answer only those statements that you feel quite certain about.

1. Although much has been written about school climate, there has yet to be available a valid and reliable instrument to measure school climate. TRUE / FALSE

2. Regardless of how school climate has been defined over the years, to a greater or lesser extent, all research on school climate finds a positive correlation between better school climate and increased student achievement. TRUE / FALSE

3. Although the literature commonly states that the school principal's leadership style is the key to establishing a positive climate in the school, specific research to support this contention has not been established. TRUE / FALSE

4. Today, the terms "climate" and "culture" are viewed as "synonyms" by authorities in the field. Conceptually, there are no differences between these terms. TRUE / FALSE

5. Trying to measure climate by the use of a questionnaire is equivalent to trying to measure the moisture in the air with a foot ruler. TRUE / FALSE

6. Research has found that feeling safe in school greatly promotes student learning and healthy development. TRUE / FALSE

7. Empirical evidence and scientific research support the contention that organizations with positive climates have heterogeneous personnel policies. TRUE / FALSE

8. Some designers of improved school principal evaluations systems are including school climate surveys as one of the many measures of principal performance. TRUE / FALSE

9. Principals, through their leadership and management practices, can determine what human, financial, material and social resources are brought to bear on schools, and how those resources are allotted. TRUE / FALSE

10. Some authorities are now recommending the use of school climate assessment as a measure of accountability. TRUE / FALSE

Climate Quiz Answers

Statements 2, 6, 7, 8, 9 and 10 are True.
Statements 1, 3, 4 and 5 are False.

Climate Quiz Scoring

10–9 correct answers: Excellent knowledge of climate concepts.

8–7 correct answers: Very good knowledge of climate concepts.

6–5 correct answers: Good knowledge of climate concepts.

4–3 correct answers: Fair knowledge of climate concepts.

2–0 correct answers: Be sure to study this chapter.

Discussion of the Climate Quiz Answers

Now, let's examine each of the statements and answers relative to the rationale for their true or false answers.

Statement 1 is false. There are indeed numerous valid and reliable instruments available for measuring school climate. Several examples of such instruments will be presented later in the chapter. Some climate instruments are to be completed by teachers, some by students and some by parents or other members of the school community. Some instruments are such that anyone can complete the climate assessment. One of the most well-known and widely utilized climate instruments is Halpin and Croft's (1962) *Organizational Climate Description Questionnaire* (OCDQ). This questionnaire was revised later and designed for use exclusively at either the elementary, the middle school or the secondary school level. For example, the revised OCDQ-RE was designed for the elementary school. It described four prototypes termed open, engaged, disengaged and closed. Each of these OCDQ instruments was tested for validity and reliability at their respective school levels.

Statement 2 is true. Numerous studies have been administered with findings that the status of the school climate indeed influences the quality of student achievement. The findings reveal that the more positive the school climate, the higher the student achievement test scores. "In sum, there is a compelling body of research that underscores the importance of school climate. Positive school climate promotes student learning, academic achievement, school success and healthy development" (NCLC, n.d., p. 7).

Statement 3 is false. The research is unanimous in underscoring the importance of the school principal's leadership for developing a positive school climate. "Leadership is the most important determinant of organizational climate" (NCLC, n.d.). Research studies have approached the topic of organizational climate from various perspectives. For example, Sweeney (1992) found that the principal's effectiveness for establishing a learning environment in the school correlated highly with a positive school climate, and the principal's human resources management was highly correlated with a positive school climate. Another study found a significant difference between the leadership style of a school principal and the subscale of school climate.

Statement 4 is false. Although the terms "culture" and "climate" tend to be used interchangeably at times and do have some similar characteristics, the terms are much different conceptually. As pointed out by Norton (2008), **culture** is more normative than climate in the sense that it is a reflection of the shared beliefs, values and underlying assumptions of school members across an array of organizational dimensions that include but go beyond interpersonal relationships. **School climate** "is the collective personality of a school. . . . It is the atmosphere that prevails as characterized by the social and professional interactions of people" (Norton, 2008).

Statement 5 is false. To the contrary, valid and reliable instruments for measuring school climate are readily available to principals for use in their schools. Several of these climate instruments will be presented later in the chapter. Clifford et al. (2012) describe thirteen valid and reliable instruments for measuring climate.

Statement 6 is true. It is clear that a safe climate fosters a positive connection with the school on the part of the students and staff, and lends to the establishment of a learning-culture environment. "Unsafe schools and inadequate facilities affect students as well as teachers. Unsafe, deteriorated, and overcrowded schools threaten the chances that students will develop social values of integrity, discipline, and civic-mindedness and allow little enthusiasm for life-long learning" (Jones et al., 2008, p. 1). Physical safety (as well as social-emotional safety) is considered to be an essential factor for establishing a learning climate in the school, according to most authorities in the field of education.

Statement 7 is true. This true statement might be somewhat surprising to you. The popular conception is that we need to have a homogeneous group of members working in the school, ones that have the same philosophy that we ourselves project. Nevertheless, Steiner's (1971) book on the creative organization points out that one primary characteristic of creative organizations is having a heterogeneous personnel policy. The creative organization has conflicting types of personalities that become mutually supporting. Each individual meets different functional requirements of the organization; order and change, stability and innovation, organizationally patterned behavior and departures from these patterns are in evidence. The creative organization purposely includes different types of people that serve as the "sparkers" who can bring unusual solutions into ongoing routines.

Statement 8 is true. Although the movement to include school climate as a factor of the school principal's performance evaluation is relatively new, it is true that the concept is gaining support in practice. "One guidepost offered by research suggests that principals influence teaching and learning by creating a safe and supporting school climate. Some designers of improved school principal performance systems are including school climate surveys as one of many measures of principal performance" (Clifford et al., 2012, p. 1). School climate can enhance or inhibit the ability of students to achieve academically. Part of the rationale for including this aspect as a factor of the school principal's performance evaluation rests on the fact that school climate, as a data-driven concept, has been shown to have so much to do with the improvement of student learning, job satisfaction, teacher retention, mutual trust, risk prevention, increased student graduation rates, and the social-emotional health of teachers and students.

The improvement of the school's climate has become an expected outcome of the school principal's human resources leadership. "Some designers of improved school principal evaluation systems are including school climate surveys as one of the many measures of principal performance. . . . We advise states and school districts to carefully study principal evaluation systems that are performing well and then select climate surveys that are useful measures of performance" (Clifford et al., 2012, p. 1).

Statement 9 is true. As the answer to statement 8 points out, the leadership style weighs heavily on the outcomes of the school climate. As pointed out throughout this chapter, school principals have opportunities for implementing leadership practices that determine and most often control what and how human resources, material resources and process resources are implemented in the school. In short, the leadership of the school principal is being viewed not only as a major responsibility, but as an outcome of the school principal's expected leadership. Most authorities and researchers in the field consider the school principal to be the key to fostering positive climate in the school.

Statement 10 is true. As stated in the answer to statement 8, the paramount importance of school climate and its influence on so many factors of quality education have connected the status of the school climate to the quality of leadership of the school principal. This perspective points out that the school principal does have control over many conditions within the school. For example, if students are not learning academically, or if relationships among students and faculty personnel are unsatisfactory, the thinking is that the principal should be held accountable.

The Significance of Developing a Healthy School Climate

Previously we told you that working to create a healthy school climate is near the top of things that you can do to improve student achievement. School climate is among the most researched topics in education. This chapter focuses on what we know about organizational climate and what the school principal must do in order to achieve it. In doing so, primary attention is given to how the school principal can foster a positive environment in the school as he or she administers the human resources function.

The topic of school climate is painted with a broad brush. Research has considered climate from the viewpoints of a safe and orderly school environment; setting high expectations for student success; positive home–school relations; establishing a clear school mission; providing instructional leadership; doing frequent monitoring of student progress; creating job satisfaction; creating mutual trust; establishing group cooperation; establishing positive teacher, student, teacher and principal relations; effective administrative leadership; maintaining positive student–peer relations; developing open communications; practicing meaningful instructional management; promoting positive human relationships; and improving other administrative practices. It is defined in the literature in numerous ways as well. Climate is high on the list of topics that have been thoroughly researched in education.

The following definition of school climate will serve the purpose of this chapter.

School climate "is the collective personality of a school. . . . It is the atmosphere that prevails as characterized by the social and professional interactions of people. . . . Climate is concerned with the process and style of a school's organizational life, rather than its content and substance" (Norton, 2008, p. 237). The definition is clear, in that climate is a people condition. The chapter begins by summarizing the findings of important research that has been conducted on the topic of school climate. Later in the chapter, the various ways to measure the school's climate are discussed, and then just how effective administration of HR processes influences the school's climate is presented.

In this chapter, the research on school climate and its effects on the HR function is discussed, measuring and assessing school climate in the school are presented, the characteristics of schools with healthy climates are detailed, how to build trust in the school environment is discussed, and tips for fostering a creative climate in your school are set forth.

School Climate Is Most Often the Difference Between Success and Failure

Much of the research on school climate has focused primarily on its influence on student academic achievement. Research results on this topic have been most positive. In summary, those schools with positive, open climates have higher student academic achievement scores. Our focus, however, is on the importance and influence of the school's climate on the HR processes and related personnel activities being administered. How does competent administration of the HR processes add to the positive quality of the school's climate?

School Climate and the HR Function: What the Research Says

School climate research related to its influence on student learning, motivation and a multitude of other physical, emotional and mental conditions has been reported in numerous publications. However, clearly one of the most exhaustive and informational publications on the topic of climate research in the literature is the *Review of Educational Research* published by AERA and SAGE (Thapa et al., 2013). This excellent, 29-page publication lists 206 references as the bases for its climate review. We recommend this reading to all practicing school principals, as well as those individuals that aspire to the role of principal.

A summary of the influences of school climate on student learning, behavior, and physical, emotional and mental health is shown in Figure 4.1. These outcomes hold important implications for the HR function in schools. For example, it seems clear that the influence of climate as related to student safety relates to the safety of teaching personnel, administrators and support staff as well. The influence of a positive school climate for reducing student absenteeism and lowering behavior problems also increases the probability of job satisfaction on the part of the professional staff.

As previously indicated, the overwhelming majority of available climate research holds implications for student outcomes. Figure 4.1 summarizes many of the positive outcomes of healthy school climates synthesized from numerous research studies.

Although findings of available climate research do hold implications for the school personnel processes as well, additional research concerning the influence of school climate on the personnel function in schools is needed.

It has been noted previously that the support of teachers by the school principal serves to increase their job satisfaction and commitment to their profession (this is reiterated later in this chapter as well). Fulton et al. (2005)

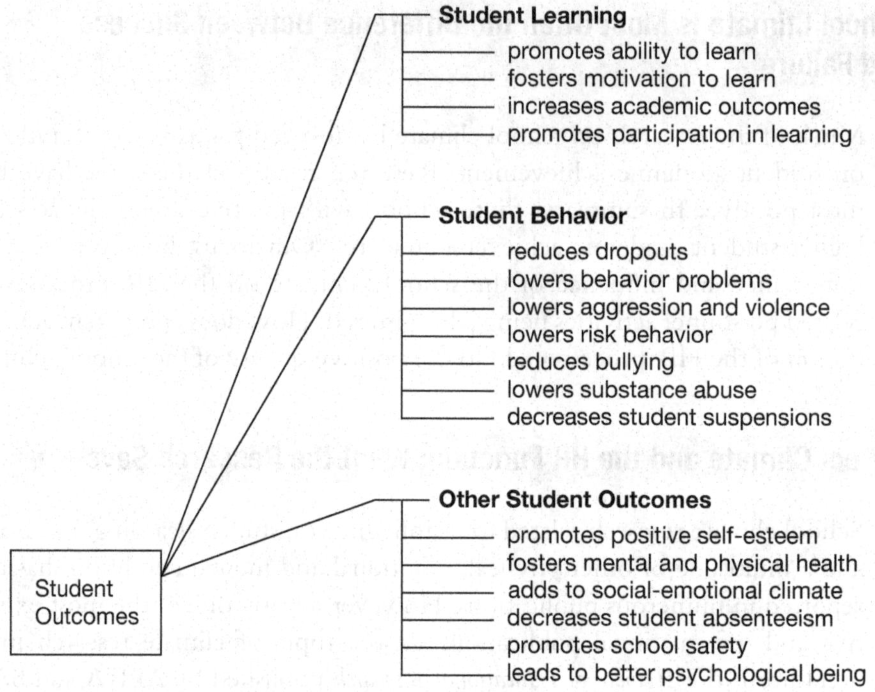

FIGURE 4.1. Outcomes of Positive School Climate on Student Learning, Behavior, and Physical, Emotional and Mental Health: What the Research Says

point out that a positive school climate has an important influence on the retention of teachers. It is clear that unsafe schools deter school personnel. Safe and caring school climates serve to foster higher levels of job satisfaction on the part of school employees. Grayson et al. (2008) report that school climate can increase or decrease the school staff's feelings relative to personal accomplishment as well as teacher retention. The National Commission on Teaching and America's Future Induction into Learning Communities submits that the induction of new teachers into education must take place in a healthy school climate (Fulton et al., 2005).

How to Measure Your School's Climate

We now have many instruments that can serve for determining the state of the climate in our schools. As previously discussed, we believe that the measurement of the climate in schools increasingly will become a required administrative activity. We no longer can argue that such assessments take too much instructional time or that the expense is prohibitive. As will be pointed out in this section, valid and reliable climate instruments are now available that take no more than 8 minutes of time to complete.

Halpin and Croft's Organizational Climate Description Questionnaire (OCDQ) in 2002 by the Center for Social and Emotional Education. The OCDQ was revised in 2008. Reportedly, the survey can be administered within a 20-minute time period. Its primary focus includes assessments relative to school safety and interpersonal relations, and it is perhaps the "grandfather" of climate instruments for use in education. The OCDQ was developed in 1962 (Halpin & Croft, 1962), and focused on the relationships among group members, and relationships between teachers and the school principal. Because the OCDQ was validated at the elementary school level, other authorities were motivated to revise the OCDQ instrument; elementary, middle school and secondary school climate instruments were developed for use at these school levels. Thus, the OCDQ-RE (Hoy & Tarter, 1997), the OCDQ-RM (Hoy & Tarter, 1997) and the OCDQ-RS (Kottkamp et al., 1987). The OCDQ-RS, for example, assesses school climate from four specific dimensions:

1. Supportive and directive behaviors of teacher personnel;
2. The behaviors exhibited by the school principal;
3. The behaviors exhibited by the school's teachers; and
4. The specific behaviors related to teachers' relationships with students, other teachers and the school's supervisors.

School Climate Measurement Tools Are Readily Available

Many other climate survey instruments are readily available to school principals. One widely used climate survey is the *Comprehensive Assessment of School Environments* (CASE) instrument available through the National Association of Secondary School Principals (NASSP). The CASE battery consists of four survey instruments. The NASSP School Climate Survey is designed to elicit responses from all major stakeholder groups (students, parents and teachers), and has three separate NASSP satisfaction surveys for each of the three major stakeholder groups. Each survey has eight to ten subscales touching on all-important aspects of the school environment. It measures data about perceptions on ten subscales, including teacher–student relationships, student behavior values, administration, student–peer relationships, parent and community cooperation, and instructional management (Lunenburg, 2011).

It is common for schools to design their own climate survey questionnaires, and the results of these surveys can be beneficial. However, such surveys are seldom checked for validity and reliability, and there are numerous climate surveys available that have been used in hundreds of school situations and then checked and re-checked for statistical validity and reliability.

Among the more recent climate instruments available for use in your school are the following.

The Gallup Q^{12} Instrument. This survey instrument is used to measure employee engagement, and reportedly can be administered in less than ten minutes. One special feature of this instrument is the fact that a high Q^{12} score exhibits lower employee turnover. The survey includes 12 questions, such as "Is there someone at work that encourages your development?"; "In the last seven days have you received recognition or praise for doing something good?"; and "In the last year, have you had opportunities to learn and grow?" Such questions focus directly on the HR process of growth and development. Source: John Thackray (2001).

Comprehensive School Climate Inventory (CSEE). The CSEE was developed for school environment. The instrument contains 10 dimensions of climate for students and parents and two additional dimensions related to the work environment for the school staff. Source: National School Climate Center (2002a): Center for Social and Emotional Education (CSEE), New York, NY. Web: www.schoolclimate.org

Teaching Empowering Leading and Learning Survey (TELL). The TELL climate instrument, reported in the 2013 Tell Kentucky survey, includes several HR questions, including one on professional development and one on new teacher support. Other questions focus on teacher leadership, school leadership, managing student conduct, instructional practices and support and other dimensions of climate. Source: New Teacher Center. Web: www.tell kentucky.org.

Organizational Climate Inventory (OCI). The OCI, developed by Hoy (2005–2013) and others (see also Hoy et al., 2002), is high on the list of frequently used instruments for assessing school climates. The OCI includes 12 behavioral norms within three cultural dimensions of constructive, passive/defensive, and aggressive/defensive. The instrument is to be completed by the teaching staff and focuses on "principal leadership, teacher professionalism, achievement press for students to perform academically, and vulnerability to the community" (Hoy, 2005–2013). Source: http://www.waynehoy.com/oci.html

The School Climate Survey Revised. According to Butler and Alberg (National School Climate Center, 2002b), the School Climate Survey Revised is one of three climate instruments that met the American Psychological Association's criteria for being a valid and reliable tool in a 2010 survey. The survey is a scientifically based set of measures that provides a comprehensive picture of a range of school climate dimensions. Among the dimensions of climate assessed are leadership, environment, order and safety. Source: National School Climate Center, New York, or call 1–866–670–6147.

The CFK Ltd. School Climate Profile. Although developed several years ago in 1973, the Charles F. Kettering School Profile published by Phi Delta Kappa (1973) is one of the most comprehensive survey instruments still available. Students, teachers and parents can complete the climate survey. It sets forth important requirements relating to program, process and material determinants of school climate. Such climate factors as caring, school renewal, teacher morale and mutual respect are assessed on a Likert-type scale. Phi Delta Kappa was one of the early educational leaders that gave attention to the importance of school climate for achieving school goals and objectives. Source: Phi Delta Kappa, Bloomington, Indiana.

The Leadership You Need to Provide to Improve and Maintain a Healthy School Climate

This section of the chapter centers primarily on how successful school principals implement and maintain a healthy climate in the school. We submit that a great deal of "how to do it" information has already been described in the previous three chapters of the book. There is no question that your professional practices concerning the implementation of the primary practices of the human resources function weigh heavily on the factors that establish the kind of school climate that fosters the positive growth and development of all learners. The HR processes are evident in some manner in every activity of the school principal as he or she works to develop a positive learning climate in the school. Research on the topic of school climate not only supports the importance of the school principal's leadership and support behaviors, but what is done at the outset of the hiring process, the orientation of new personnel, the importance of personnel assignments, supportive formative teacher performance evaluations, and staff growth and development loom significant in the successful establishment of a positive learning culture and climate in the school.

We will discuss research and practice relative to how effective principals promote a positive and creative school climate, and will also consider the importance of trust that some persons view as the foundation of a positive school climate.

Trust and Its Effects on Your School's Climate

One school principal commented, "If you lose your trust, you've lost the ballgame." His comment was an indirect way of pointing out that the evidence of positive or negative trust levels are revealed in the overall levels of achievement of the goals and objectives of the school program. It is relatively easy to lose the trust of your faculty and staff, but we submit that you can build your trust level just as easily. Here are a few tips that have proven most helpful in building trust in your school.

Tips That You Should Consider for Improving Your School's Climate

1. A way of building a reputation of trustworthiness is to be reliable and consistent in what you do and what you say. If, for some unforeseeable reason, you are unable to do what you have said you will do, be the first one to point out the reasons for not being able to keep your word. Don't make promises that you cannot deliver. It is much better to say at the outset, "I promise that I will give this my best and I do plan to deliver, but the odds are not in our favor due to (whatever)" than to simply state after the fact, "Well, I tried, but couldn't get the support I needed." Trustworthiness can only be enhanced, however, if we can do what we say we can do. If others know that you have honestly tried to keep your word, trust is elevated.

Hoy and Tschannen-Moran (1999) term this behavior "reliability"; consistency in knowing what others can expect from you. Reliability must be accompanied by truth and honesty. "I made a mistake" is a confession that most everyone will understand. Hoy and Tschannen-Moran point out that trusted administrators reveal a consistency between words and actions.

2. Be a caring person in your constant relationships with others. Think about the persons that you have known during your lifetime that you would select for your board of directors. After listing four or five persons, stop and think just why you selected them. Most likely you selected them because you knew that they cared especially about you. Unselfishly, these individuals had taken

the time and made the effort to help you pursue your strengths and improve in those areas of need. You took their advice, positive or corrective, because you trusted them. You knew that you would not be "harmed" by this trusted party; that they would always act in your best interests.

3. Your trustworthiness is revealed in part in the extent to which you accept your own accountability. It is common for us to remind our teachers, staff and students of their need to accept accountability for their assigned responsibilities, and so should you as school principal. In planning programs and school activities and making assignments for their implementation, goals and objectives, put yourself in the proper assigned position and hold yourself accountable for the results. Blaming others for the lack of success is not acceptable; understand that ultimately, the school principal is held accountable for all the program results. In one interview, the principal commented, "When we succeed, the credit is readily given to the team, when we do not meet our goals, I am the one that must be held accountable."

How to Establish a Positive Climate That Promotes Professional Growth and Fosters a Learning Culture in the School

Both empirical evidence and scientific research support a synthesis of guidelines for establishing a positive climate in your school. Figure 4.2 illustrates several guidelines that promote the establishment of a positive climate in the school. The school principal promotes a healthy climate in the school by:

1. Establishing meaningful goals and objectives that are unique to the culture of the school-community and meet the best interests and identified needs of the students.
2. Implementing an effective program of human resources administration that emphasizes planned programs for recruiting, selecting, orienting, assigning, evaluating, developing, retaining and protecting professional and staff personnel. Accomplishment of this goal is the primary theme of this book. If given high priority as part of your leadership responsibilities as principal, the results will be seen in the climate of your school.
3. Fostering personal and professional performance expectations for all school personnel and students of the school. We have never known a teacher that did not want to be a better teacher. School climate is positively influenced when opportunities are provided for employees to grow and develop.

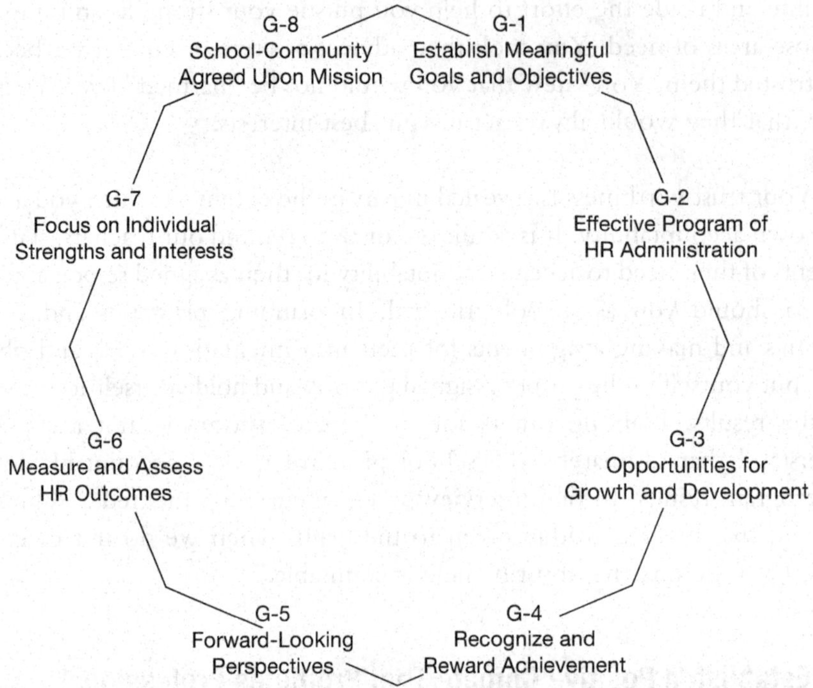

FIGURE 4.2. Guidelines for Promoting a Positive School Climate in Your School

The support of the school principal is one of the most frequently mentioned factors that foster job satisfaction and retention of personnel.

4. Recognizing and rewarding achievement of the school's success and the merit of individuals loom significant for fostering a sense of pride and satisfaction on the part of the school's faculty and staff. A personal word of appreciation takes little time but travels a long distance. "I want you to know that your contributions to our mission are essential to our future success" represents a verbal reward that is just as satisfying as a certificate of appreciation.
5. Establishing a perspective that looks toward what the school can become, as opposed to what it has been. Implementing a variety of methods for gaining new ideas for improvement based on their merit as opposed to the source of the suggestion.
6. Measuring and assessing the outcomes of the school's human resources programs and procedures relative to their accomplishment of stated objectives, including quality hires, employee retention, talent management, personal safety, and quality faculty and student performance.

7. Giving priority to the implementation of personnel strengths and interests in program assignments, and giving appropriate praise and attention for the special contributions made by both professional and support personnel. Praise is given sincerely for "thinking" and submitting ideas that are evaluated; everything is heard.
8. Implementing a personal program of ongoing growth and development. Personal competence on the part of the school principal is essential for serving as an example of what is expected on the part of every employee. The school principal is a learner along with members of the faculty. As a member of the school's improvement team, he or she shares what has been learned with all members of the team.
9. Working to develop a school community in which all stakeholders share a set of essential values set forth in a stated mission, participate in the decision-making processes of the school, and actively support the stated goals and objectives of the school's program.
10. Measuring school climate, and assessing and utilizing the results of climate surveys to reinforce the continuation of human resources provisions, or to bridge the gaps between current practices and desired outcomes, will lead to positive outcomes that permeate all of the primary functions of the school's program.

Summary

The paramount importance of leading to develop a positive school climate was the primary theme of Chapter 4. The key to fostering a climate that determines the success level of so many school programs and purposes has been found to be the school principal. Academic achievement on the part of the students, the behaviors of the school's faculty and staff, the safety of the school environment, teacher retention, growth and development results, quality performance, job satisfaction and other human resources processes are influenced positively or negatively by the status of the school climate. The chapter went so far as to say that the condition of the school climate is an indicator of the failure or success of the school principal.

Historically, planned procedures relative to measuring and assessing the climate of the school have been haphazard at best. However, today's demands for accountability have found their way into the calls for using climate results as part of the performance evaluation of the school principal; the accountability of the school principal for quality hires, teacher retention, teacher performance, personnel growth and development, and other program activities has brought the subject of school climate to the top of the performance agenda.

The literature is replete with research reports on the influence of school climate on students, teachers and performance results. Suggestions for improving the climate of the school are plentiful as well. The chapter closed by recommending several behaviors and responsibilities for the school principal relative to leadership for climate improvement. Competent administration of the human resources function in the school leads the list for climate improvement; improving one's knowledge and skills relative to the recruiting, hiring, orienting, assigning, retaining, evaluating and developing of the school's personnel is of paramount importance for effective school administration of the HR function today.

Discussion Questions

1. Take a moment and go back to Chapter 1, and then retake the two-minute quiz. Compare the quiz results with the results of your first quiz. Then give yourself a pat on the back for the improvement realized.
2. Take time to consider the quality of the human resources processes that are in place in your school. For example, how well planned and implemented are the key HR processes of recruitment, selection, orientation, assignment and others? Select one of the HR processes and list changes that you would implement in the process. Then either suggest the change to the appropriate office or implement the change yourself. Follow up the newly implemented procedures by measuring and assessing the outcomes realized.
3. Review the chapter section dealing with climate measurements. Select one of the measuring instruments described in the chapter or another instrument that is available to you and administer it as recommended. Perform an assessment, and evaluate the assessment results and report them to various school stakeholders as fits the case.

Case Studies

Case 4.1. I Know I Said That, but Things Do Change

Thomas Crockett was in the first semester as principal of Whittier Elementary School. He was one of the three finalists for the principal position and was the one endorsed by the school's teaching staff, mainly due to his stated positions on two matters relative to performance pay for teachers and student retention in grades.

During the school interviews with the three final candidates, Mr. Crockett had taken positions opposite those of the two other candidates on the aforementioned matters. In regard to performance pay for teachers, Principal Crockett stated clearly that he would take a strong stand against such a practice. He also took a strong stand on getting tough on student retention. The Whittier Teachers' Association had formally passed resolutions against performance pay and for retaining students in grade when reading scores did not meet grade level expectations. "I'll stand up and be counted on both of these measures," announced Crockett at the interview session. "I will support the teachers all along the way on these two matters," he said.

The matters of performance pay and retaining students in grade came up again in meetings of the school board. These matters had been on the discussion agenda of two previous board meetings, and, as would be expected, were discussed informally by school stakeholders throughout the school-community. When the time came for the school board to pass official policies on the two matters, Principal Crockett and other school principals were in attendance, along with representatives of the Whittier faculty and the Teachers' Association.

When the agenda of the board meeting turned to the question of performance pay for teachers, the board president asked for input from the audience on the matter. The president of the parent organization stood opposed to both propositions. A local businessman stood in favor of the pay-for-performance policy. No other member in the audience spoke for or against the two policies.

"Just one more call for input," said the board president, Mr. Gillespie. No one responded.

Both matters passed on 6 to 1 votes of the board.

The board meeting adjourned and Principal Crockett went to the parking lot. Three members of the Whittier faculty approached him and one member said, "Mr. Crockett, we are confused. In our interview session with you and the other two candidates, we recall that you were opposed to both measures that were passed tonight. You indicated that you would stand up and be counted when these measures came up."

"I know," replied Principal Crockett, "but things do change, you know."

Question:
Give serious thought to the case at hand and the aftermath of Principal Crockett's actions on the two matters. What, in your opinion, will Principal Crockett be facing during the remainder of the school year? Take the position of a faculty member at Whittier Elementary School. How are you feeling at this time after witnessing Principal Crockett's actions in this matter?

References

Clifford, M., Menon, R., Gangi, T., Condon, C., & Hornung, K., (2012). *Measuring school climate for gauging principal performance: A review of the validity and reliability of publicly accessible measures.* Washington, DC: American Institutes for Research.

Fulton, I. K., Yoon, I., & Lee, C. (2005). *Induction into learning communities.* Washington, DC: National Commission on Teaching and America's Future.

Grayson, K., Johnson, D., & Chen, R. (2008). Is firm trust essential in a trusted environment? How trust in the business context influences customers. *Journal of Marketing Research, 45*(2), 241–256.

Halpin, A. W., & Croft, D. B. (1962). *The organizational climate of schools.* Washington, DC: US Office of Education.

Hoy, W. K. (2005–2013). Organizational climate index (OCI). Retrieved from http://www.waynekhoy.com/oci.html

Hoy, W. K., Smith, P. A., & Sweetland, S. R. (2002). The development of the organizational climate index for high schools: Its measure and relationship to faculty trust. *High School Journal, 86(2)*, 38–49.

Hoy, W. K., & Tarter, C. J. (1997). *The road to open and healthy schools: A handbook for change* (Elementary and middle school ed.). Thousand Oaks, CA: Corwin Press.

Hoy, W. K., & Tschannen-Moran, M. (1999). The five faces of trust: An empirical confirmation in urban elementary schools. *Journal of School Leadership, 9*(3), 184–208.

Jones, M., et. al. (2008, April). *School climate and student achievement.* Paper between the California Department of Education and the University of California organized by the UC Davis School of Education for Applied Policy in Education.

Kottkamp R. B., Mulhern, J. A., & Hoy, W. K. (1987). Secondary school climate: A revision of the OCDQ. *Educational Administration Quarterly, 23*(3), 31–48.

Lunenburg, F. C. (2011). Comprehensive assessment of school environment (CASE): An underused framework for school climate measuring. *National Forum of Educational Administration and Supervision Journal, 29*(4). Retrieved from http://www.nationalforum.com

National School Climate Center. (2002a). *Comprehensive school climate inventory* (3rd version). New York, NY: Center for Social and Emotional Education.

National School Climate Center. (2002b). *The school climate survey revised.* New York, NY: National School Climate Center.

NCLC (National Center for Learning and Citizenship). (n.d.). *The school climate challenge: Narrowing the gap between school climate research and school climate policy, practice guidelines and teacher education policy.* A white paper presented by the National School Climate Center (NSCC), the Center for Social and Emotional Education (CSEE) and the Educational Commission of the States (ECS). Retrieved from http://www.ecs.org/html/projects Partners/nclc/docs/school-climate-challenge-web.pdf

Norton, M. S. (2008). *Human resources administration for educational leaders.* Thousand Oaks, CA: Sage.

Phi Delta Kappa. (1973). *School climate improvement: A challenge to the school administrator.* Bloomington, IN: Phi Delta Kappa.

Steiner, G. A. (1971). *The creative organization.* Chicago, IL: University of Chicago Press.

Sweeney, J. (1992). School climate: The key to excellence. *NASSP Bulletin, 76*(547), 69–73.

Thackray, J. (2001, March 15). Feedback for real. *Gallup Management Journal.* Retrieved from http://businessjournal.gallup.com/content/811/feedback-real.aspx#3

Thapa, A., Cohen, J., Guffey, S., & Higgins-D'Alessandro, A. (2013). A review of school climate research. *Review of Educational Research, 83*(3), 357–385. Published online April 19, 2013. doi:10.3102/0034654313483907

CHAPTER

5

Human Resources Administration and the Legal World of the School Principal

Primary chapter goal:

To understand the legal basis for the human resources function at the local school level, and its impact on the operations of the school and the work of the local school principal.

The legal world of the school principal is complex and difficult. Although school principals cannot be expected to be legal authorities, they must be knowledgeable of the primary legal environment in which they work, and be alert to the times when legal counsel should be contacted.

Chapter 5 centers on the federal, state and local legislation, and school policies related to the human resources function in local school settings. Several position responsibilities of the school principal concerning legal requirements are discussed. For school districts that have implemented federal education programs and are receiving federal funds, federal statutes that regulate these programs apply to all school districts in the 50 states. Federal laws extend through the human resources function from the outset of hiring to whenever the employee leaves the school system. In some cases, federal legislation gives the states some options for their implementation. However, legislation concerning the administration of the human resources function in schools (i.e., teacher tenure, professional growth, teacher dismissal, teacher evaluation, etc.)

often differs among the states. A related problem when dealing with federal and state legislative measures is the concern of frequent rule changes. School personnel often find themselves implementing a program such as performance evaluation differently from the edicts that were in place the year before.

Legal Advice Sources Tend to Differ in School Districts

The availability of legal advice for school principals differs as well. Perhaps the most common arrangement is that of having an attorney retained by the school district to give advice and guidance on legal matters. Empirically, it is not common to have the legal advice directly available to the school principal, although this, too, differs from school district to school district. In most cases, the school principal must communicate his or her legal concern to a certain office of the central school district, and that representative either reports the recommended action to the school principal or the principal is given permission to contact the legal counsel directly.

Our advice at the very outset is as follows. Your common sense will go far in helping you to act wisely on matters that have legal implications. However, acting precipitously and hoping for the best is not wise. If in doubt, get guidance on the acting matter according to the best legal counsel available to you. One school principal said that she hesitated to ask for legal advice, since others might view this as lacking knowledge on the matter at hand. Few school principals have legal backgrounds or sufficient experience to give advice on serious legal contentions. In fact, the school district's legal counsel commonly will have to spend time searching for the appropriate legal response.

As previously mentioned, the legal considerations that follow in the chapter center on the human resources function and its several processes as these are implemented at the local school level. Legislation directly related to pupil personnel services is not specifically discussed. Teacher personnel legislation relative to such matters as teachers' rights, the hiring of professional teacher personnel, the assignment of personnel, the performance of teaching personnel, sexual harassment, the suspension of teaching personnel, the dismissal of teaching personnel, drug-free workplace and others are discussed.

The Rights of School Personnel

Teachers have statutory rights that are granted by governments and contractual rights that are based on contract law. Teachers, like all American citizens, have the statutory right of freedom of speech. Related to freedom of speech is **academic freedom**. Academic freedom gives teachers the right to speak about their subject, to consider and implement new ideas in their teaching methods and to appropriate instructional materials suitable for their classes, and to recommend changes in the program areas of expertise. Academic freedom serves to allow teachers to teach according to their preferences. The courts will not interfere to assert the right of an individual to teach or work in the schools unless a person's rights are being illegally denied.

Although teachers are free to use their favored teaching methods, in all instances, teachers are advised to use good judgment in their teaching approaches. Indoctrination of students for or against certain beliefs, political practices or controversial issues is problematic. When the teacher's purpose is to give information about both sides of a controversial issue without expressing bias for one or the other, and students are permitted to participate in a free exercise of intelligence and learning, this procedure has been judged permissible. Authorities point out that only matters of public concern, not private concern, are protected. For example, if a teacher speaks out about a personal grievance against the school principal, this represents a private and not a public concern and is not a protected speech matter.

What About Freedom of Speech in School Settings?

Freedom of speech is a delicate matter, and the reporting of violations must be carefully considered. It is up to the employee filing the grievance to provide specific evidence that his or her freedom of speech has been violated. In turn, the school principal must use caution in implementing school policies related to academic freedom. In some instances, the principal finds himself or herself working between curricular policies of the school board and following the intentions of academic freedom on the part of the teacher.

It is not the purpose here to detail the analysis and steps required in the filing of a speech violation. However, "the first step in this analysis is to determine whether 'protected speech' is violated" (Glink, 2013). There are a number of factors to be considered in regard to follow-up on an employee's freedom of speech complaint, including the need to curtail conduct that is impeding the principal's ability to competently perform his or her position responsibilities.

Due Process: An Absolute

According to the Fourteenth Amendment to the Constitution of the United States, no state shall "deprive any person of life, liberty, or property without due process of law."

Before depriving any person of these rights, fair procedures must be implemented. Teachers enjoy both **procedural due process** and **substantive due process**. Procedural due process centers on procedures that are followed in cases where an individual is deprived of life, liberty or property. When an individual files a claim that he or she has been denied due process rights in regard to a purported violation, courts determine whether the person is being deprived of life, liberty or property; the individual must be given the opportunity to defend himself or herself; notice must be given to the individual that a violation is being filed; and an opportunity to be heard must be provided. The most commonly recommended procedures for a hearing are as follows:

1. An individual or group that hears the case and is an unbiased party.
2. A notification to the purported "violator" stating the intent of a hearing and the reasons for the procedures.
3. The individual being charged, in fairness, is given a chance to state why such a hearing is not appropriate.
4. The purported violator is given the opportunity to prepare and present evidence regarding the case and to have supportive witnesses, if appropriate.
5. Evidence to be presented by the opposing party is to be given to the person who is being charged.
6. Both parties have the right to have witnesses; witnesses can be cross-examined.
7. Depending on the case at hand, the hearing officer or party reaches a decision based on the evidence set forth. In school situations, it is common for the hearing officer or party to write a recommendation regarding the decision reached and submit it to the board of education. In most cases, the board is the authority that makes the final decision on actions to be taken. In court cases, the court's decision prevails.[1]

Due process commonly is implemented differently depending on state statutes and the matter at hand. For example, due process procedures for non-tenured teachers often differ from the procedures in place for tenured teachers. Also, due process procedures for matters dealing with teacher retention, substance abuse, insubordination and other violations commonly are applied differently in the many states.

Substantive Due Process

> Substantive due process . . . is relevant to the subject matter of the decision. Even though notice of offense was given, a hearing was held, and allowance of an appeal, the purported violator can argue that the decision was unfair because of the substance of the decision.
>
> (Wayne, 2004)

"'Substantive' rights are those general rights that reserve to the individual the power to possess or to do certain things, despite the government's desire to the contrary. These are rights like freedom of speech and religion" (Stanford School of Medicine, 2013). In brief, the state has to use sufficiently fair and just legal procedures before taking away the life, liberty and property of an individual. Freedom of speech and freedom of expression are examples of substantive rights. The principle of substantive due process gives the federal courts the authority to protect the fundamental rights of citizens from governmental interference, as stated in the Fifth and Fourteenth Amendments of the U.S. Constitution.

School employees are protected by both procedural and substantive due processes. The courts, lawyers and other constituents "argue" freely about the definition of substantive due process and its implementation in practice.

Teacher Selection and the Legal Consideration Relative to Highly Qualified Teachers

The NCLB (No Child Left Behind) requirements of hiring only highly qualified teachers must be implemented by all practicing school leaders. Federal requirements state that all teachers hired in public schools must be highly qualified. Hiring qualified personnel and then keeping them in the category of being highly qualified have become two of the most demanding jobs of school principals today. Although the federal regulations specify standards for highly qualified teacher programs, individual states have adopted specific procedures for implementing these programs. In this sense, the highly qualified teacher program rests on the jurisdiction of governors and state departments of education.

For example, the legal requirements for the state of Massachusetts are set forth in the following statement:

> Pursuant to M.G.L. Chapter 71, s. 38G, no person shall be eligible for employment as a teacher or professional support personnel or administrator unless s/he has been granted by the Commissioner an educator license with respect to the type of position for which s/he seeks employment. . . . Please note that this guidance relates to legal employability as outlined in M.G.L. Chapter 71, s. 38G, and 603 CMR 7.00. It does not cover the federal requirements for Highly Qualified teachers.
>
> (Massachusetts Department of Elementary and Secondary Education, 2010)

Most state regulations include requirements including Legal Requirements, Offices for Assistance, Waiver Regulations, Critical Teacher Shortage Waivers, Cautions in Hiring Practices, and Monitoring Processes Regarding Compliance Including Analyses and Reporting Procedures. Requirements for meeting the standards of highly qualified teacher include:

- **Requirements for Basic Subjects/Grades Taught**
  Teacher must:
  - Possess a Bachelors Degree.
  - Possess a state teacher's license.
  - Demonstrate subject-matter competency in each subject or grade taught.
- **Demonstration of Competency commonly includes:**
  - Passing of the state examination in the subjects to be taught.
  - Completion of the academic major or equivalent for subjects/grades.
  - Meeting of timeline for licensure renewal.
  - Must be highly qualified at time of hire.
- **The Principal's Responsibilities in regard to the highly qualified teacher (HQT) requirements:**
  - Inform teachers of federal and state HQT requirements.
  - Determine highly qualified determinations for their teachers.
  - Provide written document of requirements for each teacher and keep the record on file.
  - Support teachers in their activities to meet the HQT requirements.
  - Serve to clarify requirement differences between the state and federal HQT requirements.

The topics of highly qualified teacher and its applications in practice are not without criticism. The most serious criticism centers on the contention that HQT is flawed in that it sends the least qualified teachers to those schools and school districts that need the highest qualified personnel; classrooms that have the most children from low-income families and other students with special needs are being taught by personnel that are only in the process of becoming a highly qualified teacher. According to a report by Strauss (2013):

> A 2012 study from Stanford University concludes that nationally students of color in low-income schools are 3 to 10 times more likely to have teachers who are uncertified, not fully prepared, or teaching outside their field of preparation than students in predominately white and affluent schools.

Our intention here is not to argue against HQT program efforts, but to point out that such programs often are controversial, and school principals are faced with working and dealing with matters of this kind.

There is evidence that school districts are making efforts to address teacher-quality gaps among schools. For example, a Stanford University report notes three specific efforts to improve teacher assignments. State legislation has been passed to give principals in low-performing schools greater authority in the hiring of personnel for position openings, providing certain incentives for teachers to enter education and accept assignments in low-performing schools, and giving salary bonuses to teachers with certain educational qualifications to teach in schools that are having difficulties in recruiting and hiring teacher personnel (Koski & Horng, 2007).

Sexual Harassment: Is It Out of Control in the Schools?

It would be most difficult to find a school district that did not have an adopted policy on the matter of sexual harassment. Numerous studies have been conducted in school settings revealing the high incidence of sexual harassment in America's schools. This section of the chapter does not deal directly with student sexual harassment; rather, it focuses on the topic from the employee perspective, and the school principal's role in dealing with the matter.

The American Association of University Women (AAUW, 1993) conducted a study of 1,532 boys and girls in grades 8–11 in 79 public schools, and found that 83 percent of the girls and 60 percent of the boys had experienced sexual harassment in school. This study was conducted more than 10 years ago, and sexual harassment levels in schools today have decreased to approximately 50 percent, according to the AAUW (Koebler, 2011). Yet no one would accept the reported lower statistic as being satisfactory.

Sexual harassment is defined by Title VII of the Civil Rights Act of 1964 as unwelcomed sexual advances, requests for sexual favors, or other verbal or physical contact of a sexual nature. However, sexual harassment now has been viewed from two different perspectives: quid pro quo harassment, and hostile-environment harassment. **Quid pro quo** harassment is viewed as unwelcome sexual advances; requests for sexual favors; and other verbal, nonverbal or unwanted physical contact. If a school principal told a certain teacher that he would give them a good performance report if the person would give him a sexual favor, this would exemplify a quid pro quo harassment violation.

Hostile-environment harassment occurs when a supervisor or co-worker in the school establishes an environment in the workplace that is abusive to one or more other employees. Such unwelcomed behavior can be either or both verbal or physical. Unwanted touching on the job, off-color jokes, vulgar language, pornography, degrading comments and sexual innuendos are kinds of behaviors that foster a work environment that leads to the inability of some employees to perform their work and feel safe on the job.

Figure 5.1 is an example of a typical school district policy on sexual harassment. Note that the policy includes the district's definition of sexual harassment, the actions that the school board will take in case of violations, and the

---

Inappropriate sexual conduct will not be tolerated and may constitute sexual harassment. The school system does not condone or tolerate any form of sexual harassment involving employees or students. The school system is committed to the creation and maintenance of a learning and work environment in which all persons who participate in school programs and activities can do so in an atmosphere free of sexual harassment.

The school system will take appropriate action to prevent and correct behavior that violates this policy. If necessary, the school system will also take disciplinary action against employees and students. Employees who violate the policy will be subject to such actions as oral or written reprimand, professional counseling, reassignment, demotion, suspension or termination.

It is the responsibility of every supervisor to recognize acts of sexual harassment and take necessary action to ensure that such instances are addressed swiftly, fairly and effectively. The school system prohibits retaliation against an individual who reports or cooperates with an investigation of a reported incident.

FIGURE 5.1. School Board Policy on Sexual Harassment: A Policy Summary

responsibilities of school principals and every other supervisor for recognizing and dealing with acts of sexual harassment.

Principals do have guidance in the form of school board policy for dealing with the matter of sexual harassment in their school. The board policy should be discussed periodically with all members of the school staff. As school principal, you need to know what sexual harassment is and how to recognize it. You might want to include appropriate sexual harassment questions in your periodic school climate survey. The following model gives some guidance for administering the sexual harassment policy in your school. The model in Figure 5.2 recommends four definite administrative procedures for you to implement:

- Gaining a knowledge of sexual harassment, how it occurs and the federal, state and local board policies that govern harassment in schools;
- Disseminating the information regarding sexual harassment to all employees and parents in the school-community;
- Implementing the sexual harassment procedures in regard to employee responsibilities; and
- Controlling the implementation by handling violations swiftly and appropriately.

Teacher Dismissal or Suspension

Teacher dismissal or suspension commonly is due to misconduct, immorality, insubordination, incompetency or willful neglect of duty. Misconduct includes a variety of improper behaviors on the part of the teacher, including knowingly failing to report suspected child abuse. All states have statutes that regulate the termination or suspension of school personnel. Although state statutes do require similar procedures for dismissing or suspending a teacher, they do differ as well. The key recommendation for school principals who must deal with dismissal or suspension is to follow the state statutes and school board policies on these matters to the letter, while seeking the services of legal counsel. Cases of teacher dismissal and suspension often are lost by the school district, on the basis of overlooking a specific procedure in the law. Even though the principal has sufficient evidence and has been fair in his or her actions in a dismissal or suspension case, an error in procedures will be problematic. When this occurs, the attempt to terminate a teacher most likely will be set aside by the court or hearing official.

Gain Knowledge of Sexual Harassment and How It Occurs

Be Knowledgeable of Title VII and Title IX of the Civil Rights Act.

Understand the Kinds of Behavior That Accompany Unwanted Sexual Behavior.

Consider Each Observed and/or Reported Evidence of Sexual Harassment as a Serious Matter to Be Swiftly Attended.

Examine the Research on Sexual Harassment in Schools Relative to Findings About Which Employees Are Victims of Sexual Harassment.

Be Fully Aware That Violated Employees Might Not Be Ready and Willing to Report Sexual Harassment Violations That Have Been Perpetrated Upon Them.

↓

Disseminate Information Regarding Sexual Harassment to All Employees and Parents

Hold In-Service Discussions on the Policies and Regulations That Govern Sexual Harassment in the School.

Discuss With Faculty and Support Personnel the Behaviors That Constitute Sexual Harassment.

Include the Topic of Sexual Harassment in the School's Orientation Process, Especially With New Employees.

↓

Implement the Sexual Harassment Procedures in Relation to Each Employee's Responsibility

Train the School's Department Heads, Secretarial Assistants and Other Support Staff Supervisors Relative to the Policies and Regulations for Sexual Harassment Violations, and Help Them to Realize Their Leadership Responsibilities in This Regard.

Establish an Appropriate Procedure for Filing a Sexual Harassment Complaint Either Verbally or in Writing.

Assure All Employees That Complaints for Sexual Harassment Violations Will Remain Confidential and Do Not Let This Assurance Be Violated.

↓

Control the Implementation by Handling Violations Swiftly and Appropriately

As School Principal, Be Certain That All Violation Complaints Are Seriously Considered and Handled Swiftly.

Control the Privacy of the Person Filing the Complaint, but Also Protect the Rights of the Person or Persons That Have Been Accused.

Be Absolutely Certain to Keep a Detailed Record of the Violation Complaint and Accurate Records of Follow-Up Procedures and Findings.

Implement Discipline Procedures Strictly According to the School District Harassment Policy and Federal and State Legislation That Might Apply.

Use Appropriate Measures to Protect School Employees From Sexual Harassment Instigated by Outside-of-School Parties.

FIGURE 5.2. Administrative Procedures for School Principals Regarding the Administration of Sexual Harassment

Suspension and/or Dismissal: The Importance of the Due Process Hearing

Suspension commonly is viewed as the release of a teacher from duty for a specified period of time due to a violation of school policies and procedures or one of the aforementioned violations. It is consider as a "lay off" of professional personnel, often prior to a dismissal hearing, especially if the teacher's conduct is potentially harmful to the school's students. In most states, a temporary suspension of 3 to 5 days can be administered without the necessity of a hearing on the case. However, if a teacher is suspended for more than ten days, state statutes most often call for a due process hearing.

In most cases, the school board appoints an impartial personnel hearing officer to conduct a suspension hearing. The hearing procedures are quite similar to any due process hearing:

1. A written notice of the charge or charges is given to the employee;
2. Due process calls for a fair hearing before an impartial hearing officer, most often selected by the school board;
3. The employee commonly is given the opportunity to be represented by counsel;
4. An opportunity for both parties to have witnesses is provided (i.e., school representatives and employee witnesses);
5. Cross-examination of all witnesses is provided; and

6. It is common to have all testimony given under oath.

The hearing officer prepares a written report of the hearing proceedings, and presents his or her findings and recommendations to the board of education. The school board is the official body that makes a final decision regarding the case at hand. In many cases, the findings result in a further suspension pending an official hearing for dismissal in the court or other authoritative educational body in the district, county or state. Findings of the school board usually are delivered to the employee within ten days of the hearing. Dismissal cases generally follow the same report-back timetable.

Procedures for the dismissal of teachers are quite different for tenured and non-tenured personnel. In some states, a non-tenured teacher can be dismissed on or before a specified time, generally of three years. Tenured teachers are considered to have property rights, and these rights cannot be violated without due process of law. Whenever the school principal submits a written statement of an employee's charges of violations that are alleged to necessitate dismissal, the school superintendent presents a statement of the charges to the governing board. In turn, the governing board adopts an official statement of the case and the charges incurred to the state board of education. If the case involves certain violations that are detrimental to students, the teacher usually is placed on temporary leave or reassigned within the school district. Notices in these cases are required to be in writing and sent to the employee by registered or certified mail, addressed to the employee's last known address.

Once again, the legal statutes within each state predict the follow-up procedures for handling dismissal cases. The employee is notified of the charges in detail. In some cases, the teacher is given notice that he or she will be dismissed within a specified time period or at the close of the school year. If the teacher requests a hearing on the dismissal charges, the due process procedures come into play.

The obvious responsibilities of the school principal in cases of teacher suspension or dismissal include the matters of comprehensive and accurate documentation of the employee's actions and behaviors. Specifics of the violations, dates and times, witness reports as appropriate to the case, administrative actions taken to remedy and or improve the reported employee's behaviors and other evidence that will loom important in any hearing or court case are essential.

In addition, the school principal must follow the school district's own policies and procedures in administering personnel processes. For example, consider the case of one teacher who was under dismissal proceeding for being unfair to slow learners in his classes, walking away from parents that were questioning his treatment of some students and being an underperforming teacher. In the process of the hearing on this case, the hearing officer asked about the teacher's classroom performance evaluations. The principal stated that his performance evaluations were consistently lower than those of other members of the faculty. The hearing officer noted that all performance categories on the teacher's evaluation reports were scored under number 3, satisfactory. Only one category, appearance, was scored as being good. The hearing officer concluded that the ratings of satisfactory were at least average, and that satisfactory indicates an acceptable rating. He also pointed out that a rating of average implied that 50 percent of the school's staff could be below the charged employee's scores. The school superintendent commented that, "Well, we mean that the teacher's performance has not met our professional expectations for teachers in our school system and that his professional growth has not met our expectations." The school district's professional growth policy indicated that so many hours of university credit had to be earned within each five years of service. The employee had earned a Master's degree and had additional hours of credit during the required time period that far surpassed the school district's growth requirements. Little or no counseling had been given to the teacher in relation to his relationships with parents or with students. The hearing officer's report to the school board noted each of these performance factors, and asked for a dismissal of the case, not the dismissal of the employee.

The implications of the foregoing case are clear. Giving feedback to an underperforming teacher is a difficult task. School policies and administrative regulations are of great importance when making personnel performance evaluations. Our "kindness" tends to inhibit our ability to give low scores, even though we know that such ratings are deserved in some cases. Since we sometimes have difficulty giving scores of 1 or 2, a rating of 3 is given instead. After all, we argue, a rating of 3 is below the ratings of most other teachers. Objective performance evaluations are part of the accountability responsibilities of the school principal, and loom significant in matters related to teacher competence in the classroom.

The advice to keep in mind regarding the intended dismissal of a teacher centers on being certain that the individual has been fully informed of his or her unsatisfactory performance, and has been instructed as to the areas of needed improvement. In addition, hearing officers and/or the courts are certain to ask the question, "What has been done to help the teacher improve in the areas of need?"

Drug-Free Workplace

In 1988, the federal government passed the Federal Drug-Free Workplace Act. The act requires that federal contractors and grantees—including school districts—that receive more than $25,000 in federal funds be drug-free, and initiate policies that notify all employees that the workplace environment is to be drug-free and that this condition is a requirement of employment. Drug and alcohol policies in school systems have focused primarily on substance abuse on the part of students. In regard to school employees, the primary concern has focused on the question of whether the use of drugs has inhibited the fitness of the teacher or support employee in his or her job performance. Previously, possession of drugs alone has not been the basis for teacher suspension or dismissal.

In the past, a school board most likely would not suspend a teacher for the possession of marijuana unless specific evidence revealed that competence in classroom instruction was being negatively affected. Now, however, the approval of the use of medical marijuana presents new concerns for school principals. If a teacher's physician has prescribed the drug, what does this mean in regard to the teacher's use of it on a daily basis? The answer to this question was given by the California Supreme Court in the case of *Ross v. RagingWire Telecommunications, Inc.* (2008).

In the aforementioned court case, Ross had been refused employment in the telecommunications company due to his use of medical marijuana for back problems.

The California Supreme Court not only upheld the existing laws that allow an employer to terminate an employee for medical marijuana use, but implied that California cannot legislate around federal law to require employers to tolerate medical marijuana use. The Ross decision was instrumental in clarifying that California employers are not required to accommodate or permit marijuana use by their employees, even marijuana that may be covered by the Compassionate Use Act (see Liebert Cassidy Whitmore, 2008). The California Supreme Court decision also affirmed laws that can require pre-employment drug tests and can take illegal drug use into consideration in making employment decisions. Although the case was a California ruling, such case law goes far in determining rationale for decisions by other courts in other states on the same subject.

In summary, historically, court decisions have not supported the dismissal of teachers if convicted of the possession of marijuana or other drugs, but the courts would likely support a teacher's termination with evidence that showed that drugs were inhibiting the quality of classroom instruction required for positive student learning.

That's Insubordination! No, That's Freedom of Speech

Insubordination on the part of a school faculty or support staff member is viewed as the unwillingness to follow the specific directions set forth by an authority, or the refusal to obey the policies, administrative procedures and orders of the school board, superintendent, principal or other supervisor to whom the employee is responsible. But is the response to an order by the employee insubordinate, or is it simply the employee's freedom of speech? One guideline for determining the difference between insubordination and freedom of speech is that of reasonableness.

Snapshot 1

The principal asks for the faculty members' opinions on the new plan. Melanie Morton, a sixth-grade teacher, sends a memo to the principal indicating that research on the topic of student retention points out that student retention is not in the best interests of students. In fact, retention in grade results in more problems than it solves. She stated that the available research on student retention should be reviewed before any such plan is implemented. The principal requests that Miss Morton come to the office after school. At the meeting, the principal states that Miss Morton's comments in her memo were evidence of insubordination.

Was the teacher insubordinate? Not in this case. Teachers were asked to give their opinion of the principal's plan for student retention, and Miss Morton did so. Her memo was not disrespectful, nor was there any evidence that the teacher willfully disobeyed an order. If, perhaps, the teacher's memo had stated that the plan for student retention was flawed, and that she, as a professional, would absolutely not follow the plan if implemented, insubordination most likely would have been in evidence.

It is clear that the definition of insubordination accepted by the court looms important in its rulings. In some cases, insubordination has been considered as narrow grounds for teacher dismissal. In other case rulings, insubordination was viewed as the failure of the employee to follow expressed or implied directions or reasonable orders. Not following or obeying a school board's policy statement most likely would be considered as not following an implied direction. Or if specific directives were specifically disobeyed, insubordination would most likely be in evidence. An adopted policy of the school board is a legal statement that hearing officers and the courts view as an official directive.

Cases in which the teacher refused to adopt a professional growth plan have been ruled in courts to be insubordination. In one instance, a school principal asked a teacher to explain his procedure for grading students. The teacher simply referred the principal to a page in the school's handbook. Insubordination was upheld. Refusal to sign in each morning according to the principal's directives has resulted in insubordination reports, and the charge has been upheld by the courts.

A directive given by a school principal must meet the criterion of reasonableness. Empirical evidence suggests that the only time that a faculty or staff member should refuse to follow a directive is when the directive would endanger the employee's health, safety or the safety of others. In any case, legal counselors always recommend that the employee should "follow the directive first, and grieve later."

Other Important HR Legislation That You Need to Know

As noted by Wikipedia (2013), for any organization to have an efficient ability to grow and advance, human resources is key. Human resources administration is viewed as a system's structure that gives assurance that public service staffing is accomplished in an unbiased, ethical and values-based manner. We view this passage as important for school principals to understand. It underscores the essence of the human resources function in education.

This book has pointed to numerous legislative statutes that pertain to the effective administration of the human resources function in schools. Summaries of selected major laws that govern human resources administration in the public sector are presented in this section.

Title VII of the Civil Rights Act of 1964

This law prohibits discrimination in hiring, compensation, and terms and conditions of employment on the basis of race, color, religion, national origin or sex. The act was extended in 1972 to include employees of state and local governments and educational institutions (see Equal Employment Opportunity Act, 1972). Problems in the area of equal opportunity continue to exist. Two approaches have been implemented in an attempt to remedy equal opportunity problems. One effort has been to use the "color blind" approach that treats every individual equally regardless of various differences. A second approach has been the implementation of affirmative action, whereby organizations were encouraged to hire people based on their color, age, gender and so forth, purportedly to make up for discrimination that has taken place historically. The concept of affirmative action has been met with strong opposition, with opponents indicating that the persons with the highest qualifications for the position should be hired regardless of color, race, gender and other characteristics.

Section 504 of the Rehabilitation Act of 1973

This law prohibits discrimination against any individual on the basis of their disability. The requirements of the act apply to any organization that receives federal funds from any federal department or agency. The term "disability" is defined as referring to any person with a physical or mental impairment that substantially limits one or more life activities. To deny a person with disabilities employment, the employing agency must present strong evidence that the disabled person could not perform the requirements of the position in question.

In most instances, the hiring agency would be required to take all possible means to make reasonable accommodations for the person with disabilities to work effectively in the job. If the hiring agency could demonstrate that the requirements of the position would prove unsafe for the disabled person or other persons working in the same environment, not hiring the individual might be approved. However, the U.S. Equal Opportunity Commission most likely would require the employing agency to demonstrate the safety claims.

The Pregnancy Discrimination Act of 1978

This law prohibits sex discrimination on the basis of pregnancy. Section 701 of the Civil Rights Act of 1974 was amended by adding that the references to sex in the original act include, but are not limited to, discrimination because of or on the basis of pregnancy, childbirth, or related medical conditions. Employees who are pregnant are to be treated the same as other persons for all employment-related purposes. The act details additional provisions for pregnancy in relation to fringe benefits and how certain insurance and collective bargaining provisions are to be administered.

The Immigration Reform and Control Act of 1986

This law was passed as an effort to resolve the immigration problems being faced at that time. The act set forth several specific requirements:

1. Employers were required to attest to their employees' immigration status.
2. Employers could not knowingly hire or even recruit unauthorized immigrants.
3. Legal status was given to immigrants who entered the US before January 1, 1982 if they had resided in the country.
4. Legal status was given to certain illegal immigrants that worked seasonally in the country. Approved legal status was dependent on the immigrants' ability to prove that they were not guilty of crimes, and they had to be knowledgeable of U.S. history, government and the English language.

The sanctions of the immigration act were to apply only to employers that had more than three employees and had made noticeable effort to determine the legal status of the workers that had been employed by them. Problems of illegal immigration remain present today, and the question of illegal immigrant children in America's schools remains in the minds of practicing school administrators.

The Family and Medical Leave Act

This law entitles eligible employees to take unpaid, job-protected leave for specified and medical reasons, and provides for the continuation of group health insurance coverage under the same terms and conditions as if the employee had not taken leave. Leave considerations include:

1. A specified leave period of 12 months for childbirth and care of the newborn child within one year of the birth.
2. The placement of an adopted child or foster child with the employee and care for 12 months within one year of the adoption.
3. Spousal care, childcare, or parent care in cases of serious health conditions.
4. Personal and serious health conditions that inhibit the ability of the employee to perform the essential functions of the job.
5. Any other qualifying condition that is based on the fact that the employee's spouse, son, daughter, or parent is a covered military member on "covered active duty." Additionally, twenty-six workweeks of leave are granted to an employee during a single 12-month time period to care for a covered service member who has had a serious injury or illness. The employee must be the spouse, son, daughter, parent or next of kin of the covered service member in order to receive military caregiver leave.

There are, of course, other federal and state legislative statutes that apply to practices of the human resources function in schools. The time and effort spent by the school principal to become acquainted with these measures will serve them in a positive way. It is not that the principal has to be highly knowledgeable about each of the statutes that have implications for the administration of HR processes; rather, being informed that a particular law has been passed serves a good purpose. If and when a specific situation occurs, knowing that information on the matter is available, or knowing that you need legal advice will serve you well.

Summary

The school principal's leadership in the legal world was the main theme of Chapter 5. Federal, state and local statutes and policies relating to the human resources processes in education are extensive. School principals need to realize that most requirements of law are established to ensure that the rights of each individual are protected in a fair and equitable manner.

The rights of every citizen to life, liberty and the pursuit of happiness underscore the importance of implementing this creed when working in a people environment such as a local school. The freedom to teach in a safe school environment is what you want and must work to provide for students, faculty and support personnel. Knowing and understanding the need to eliminate problems of sexual harassment, bullying and other disruptions of an effective learning environment require the priority attention of the school leader.

Due process is an employee's assurance that you and the school district authorities will give them a fair opportunity to give their side of the story in case of a purported violation. Trust is dependent in large part on just how well the school principal carries out this right.

Demands for improvements in school academic performance also entail the need for hiring and retaining high quality teachers. It has been said that if there is an unqualified teacher in your school, then there is an unqualified administrator in the principal's office. Your HR recruitment, hiring, assigning, orienting, evaluating and development practices and procedures are the avenues available to you for building a highly qualified staff.

Your legal world demands your knowledge of the requirements for dealing with such matters as sexual harassment, teacher dismissal and suspension, drug abuse and other problems that infiltrate the walls of the school. Several important pieces of legislation dealing with such matters were presented in the chapter. Knowing their content and requirements and being fully aware that you should seek legal guidance on many of these matters will serve you well. The principal who keeps abreast of these and other legislative matters will be appreciated by others for their leadership in dealing with and resolving problems in the school environment.

Discussion Questions

1. The two kinds of due process were discussed in the chapter. Describe the protections provided by each of them for the school employee. Consider the implications for the school principal in regard to due process as it applies to the various human resources processes such as hiring, assignment and performance evaluation.
2. What two or three aspects of the legal world of the school principal are most apparent in your school situation or in a school with which you

are most familiar? That is, what legal considerations appear to be most prevalent in the daily work of the school principal today?

3. Consider the need for the school principal to keep abreast of the many local, state and federal laws and policies that influence his or her work responsibilities. What avenues does the principal have for keeping up-to-date on the legal requirements facing him or her?

Case Studies

Case 5.1. In-Service Program Attendance Is a Waste of My Time, and I Don't Intend to Participate

Tom Black was an industrial arts teacher at the Whittier Middle School. His performance ratings during his five years at Whittier were rated in the upper 25 percent of the ratings for all teachers in the school. Tom had completed a Master's degree with a major in educational administration and policy studies last year, and had been selected by the faculty of the school as representative to the school's site-based council.

Tom's principal, Alice Walker, sent him a memo indicating that she wanted him to participate in an upcoming in-service program sponsored by the school district office on the topic of parental involvement in school programs. Tom replied to the request by answering the memo indicating that he did not choose to accept the responsibility; that he had found the last two in-service programs he had attended to be "pretty much a waste of time."

In turn, the principal went to Tom's classroom during his preparation period and requested that he meet with her after school to discuss the in-service program matter. She pointed out that the program was being sponsored by parent–teacher organizations throughout the school district, and that the school board had passed a resolution indicating the importance of the event.

"I would expect you to attend," she said.

Tom replied, "No, I don't think so. I've already said that I do not choose to participate and meeting to discuss the matter further really would not change my mind."

Principal Walker reminded Tom that he was the school's representative to the site-based council, and that parental involvement was one of the council's important concerns.

No further discussion about the in-service event took place, and on the date of the in-service event, Tom did not attend.

Question:
Review the chapter's section on insubordination. Do you believe that the school principal has evidence of insubordination in this case? If you were in the position as principal of the school, would you most likely file an insubordination complaint against Tom? Why, or why not?

Note

1. This hearing procedure is presented as a fair procedure for school districts and school principals to follow, and not as a legal requirement. State statutes often set forth the specific hearing procedures that must be implemented in due process cases.

References

American Association of University Women (AAUW). (1993). *Hostile hallways: The AAUW survey on sexual harassment in America's schools.* Washington, DC: AAUW.

Education laws and regulations. (2010). Massachusetts Department of Elementary and Secondary Education. *Mass.gov.* Retrieved from http://www.doe.mass.edu/news/news.aspx?id=5685

Equal Employment Opportunity Act. (1972). Enacted by the Senate and House of Representatives of the United States of America in Congress Assembled. Washington, DC.

Glink, S. E. (2013, November 20). Teacher and staff constitutional rights. Retrieved from http://educationrights.com/teacherconstitutionalrights.php

Koebler, J. (2011, November 9). Survey: Nearly half of students sexually harassed in school. *U.S. News & World Report.* Retrieved from http://www.usnews.com/education/blogs/high-school-notes/2011/11/09/survey-nearly-half-of-students-sexually-harassed-in-school

Koski, W., & Horng, E. (2007). Facilitating the teacher quality gap? Collective bargaining agreements, teacher hiring and transfer rules, and teacher assignment among schools in California. *Education Finance and Policy*, *2*(3), 262–300.

Liebert Cassidy Whitmore. (2008, April 17). *Ross v. Ragingwire* revisited: California Supreme Court holds that employers need not accommodate an employee's medicinal marijuana use. Retrieved from http://www.lcwlegal.com/68749

Montgomery County Public Schools. (2013). Sexual harassment policy. Adopted in November, 1992. Board of Education, Rockville, MD. Retrieved from http://www.montgomeryschoolsmd.org/info/sexualharassment

Ross v. RagingWire Telecommunications, Inc., 42 CAL.4TH 920 original opinion (2008).

Strauss, V. (2013, August 27). How the public is deceived about 'highly qualified teachers.' *The Washington Post*. Retrieved from http://www.washingtonpost.com/blogs/answer-sheet/wp/2013/08/27/how-the-public-is-deceived-about-highly-qualified-teachers/

Stanford School of Medicine. (2013). Substantive due process. *Stanford.edu*. Retrieved from http://forensicpsychiatry.stanford.edu/Files/Substantive%20Due%20Process.htm

Wayne, R. H. (2004). Legal guidelines for dismissing students because of poor performance in the field. *Journal of Social Work Education*, *40*(3), 403–414.

Wikipedia. (2013, December 2). Public administration. Retrieved from http://en.wikipedia.org/wiki/Public_administration

CHAPTER

6

How the School Principal Can Actively Lead the Support Staff of the School

Primary chapter goal:

To increase the knowledge and skill of the school principal relative to the human resources function as it applies to classified employees.

Just Who Constitutes the Classified Staff of the Local School?

The most common response to the question that headlines this opening section is the custodian, secretarial staff, and cafeteria workers. Yet one school in the West Contra Costa School District in Richmond, California lists sixty-four jobs within its several classified job families. Common job families include secretarial and clerical personnel, instructional and library-media aides, security officers, transportation staff, food services, maintenance and facilities, and custodial workers. Not all of the sixty-four job titles are present at the local school level, but maintenance and facilities upkeep/repair, clerk/secretarial, food service, and instructional/service aide and assistant classified job titles are commonly found at all local schools today.

Finding the common ground relative to the school principal's human resources responsibilities for classified personnel is nearly impossible. Although many of the classified personnel of various job families are present in most local schools, either full or part-time, just how they are hired and assigned, just who provides classified employee orientation, and who serves as the classified employee's immediate supervisor vary greatly from school district to school district. This is just to say that no single organizational arrangement fits all. For example, in one school district, the school principal might serve as the performance evaluator for all school secretaries and educational assistants, but might not be responsible to serve as the evaluator for custodians and school nurses. The principal frequently is not the designated performance evaluator for cafeteria workers in his or her school; evaluation is left to the cafeteria manager. In other school situations, a school operations manager, maintenance supervisor, custodial coordinator, or other district office administrator is responsible for performance evaluations of respective classified workers.

One Tennessee school district's classified employee handbook stated that the school principal was the immediate supervisor of all certificated personnel and also was the immediate supervisor of all school secretaries, educational assistants, custodians and other employees at their school, but went on to say that the school cafeteria manager was the immediate supervisor of the school's food services personnel and the maintenance personnel were under the immediate supervision of the maintenance supervisor.

The purpose here is not to criticize any school district's organizational arrangement of the classified personnel program; rather, the purpose is to point out the impossibility of providing a specific model for the organization of the classified personnel program for all schools at the local level. Variations of the organizational arrangements in the administration of the classified personnel function make it virtually impossible to set forth a common model for administering the HR function at the local school level. Nevertheless, the nature of the classified human resources function in schools, and how it is both similar to yet different from the certificated HR function, is presented in the following sections.

A Classified Personnel Pre-Quiz

Check your answer for each of the questions in the following pre-quiz. Don't just guess the answer; only answer those questions for which you are quite certain.

1. What percentage of classified personnel typically constitute the total school district staff? ____ 5% to 9%; ____ 10% to 14%; ____ 15% to 19%; ____ 20% to 30%.

2. Statistics reveal that ______% of classified personnel leave their position in the school district after the first year of service. ____ 5% to 11%; ____ 12% to 17%; ____ 18% to 23%; ____ 24% to 29%; ____ more than 30%.

3. Under the Equal Employment Opportunity Act of 1972, classified personnel have the same tenure protections as certificated personnel. ____ True, or ____ False.

4. With the exception of supervisory classified personnel, classified personnel such as clerical workers, custodial employees and cafeteria workers are paid: ____ individually by a weekly salary schedule; ____ individually by a monthly salary schedule; ____ on a salary schedule that includes a base salary amount plus an increment for experience; ____ hourly wages based on job grade and years of experience.

5. Due to the nature of their jobs, custodians, bus drivers, and lunchroom workers are among several job families that do not have written job descriptions. Rather, these workers commonly are given "daily work sheets" that set out the day's work tasks. ____ True, or ____ False.

6. Since the primary responsibility of the school principal is that of certificated personnel, classified personnel at local school sites are supervised and evaluated by a central district office administrator. ____ True, or ____ False.

7. Classified personnel depend primarily on job orientation information regarding growth and development plans given to them at the time they apply by the job recruiter. ____ True, or ____ False.

8. Empirical evidence suggests that there are two primary responsibilities of local school principals concerning classified personnel at their school sites. One is to send an absence report to the central office once each month, and a second is to report classified job openings to the central human resources office. ____ True, or ____ False.

9. Classified personnel are those employees in a school position that does not require state certification. ____ True, or ____ False.

10. The term "job family" refers to all the employees (custodians, clerical workers, lunchroom workers, etc.) that serve together as a team at one local school site. ____ True, or ____ False.

Pre-Quiz Answers

Answers are ones that represent the majority of practices, and exceptions are possible.

1. Number 1 is **20% to 30%.** The statistic represents that of the school district overall; the percentage at the local school level would be

somewhat lower. In any case, in a school with 20 certificated employees, 4 to 6 of them commonly would be classified personnel.

2. Number 2 is **more than 30%.** In fact, empirical evidence indicates that between 30% and 50% of classified personnel leave the job after the first year. One primary reason given for leaving is for a job in business or industry for a larger salary. The high rate of turnover inhibits the school's ability to stabilize the workforce. Thus, employee retention becomes a major concern of the school principal.
3. Number 3 is **false.** Only certificated personnel hold tenure by law. The large majority of classified workers are on one-year-only contracts. Some classified personnel that are in supervisory positions do have contracts that are longer than one year.
4. Number 4 is **hourly wages based on job grade and years of experience.** We need to point out that there is a variety of classified employees that work at different times on different schedules. For example, there are temporary employees, substitute employees, full-time employees, part-time employees, part-time employees for business purposes, student workers and other titles. Wages for these individuals commonly are on an hourly basis and sometimes not according to a specific job grade level.
5. Number 5 is **false.** Although it most likely is true that some classified workers in schools and school districts do not have job descriptions, most school districts that have classified employee workbooks include position descriptions for every classified employee job title.
6. Number 6 is **false.** During interviews, we found no school principal that did not complete a performance evaluation for all classified employees at his or her school site. School principals supervised classified personnel as well. This is not to imply that school district personnel did not cooperate with the school principal in the administration of almost every HR process; they especially did so relative to employees in-service workshops and other development activities.
7. Number 7 is **false.** Although some orientation information is given at every HR process procedure, the school principal provides the leadership activities for both certificated and classified personnel assigned to his or her school.
8. Number 8 is certainly **false.** The school principal serves as the daily and ongoing supervisor of classified personnel in his or her school. Virtually all of the supervisory activities that the school principal does in relation to certified personnel are also done in relation to classified personnel assigned to his or her school.

9. Number 9 is basically **true.** We use the term "basically true," since it could be that some states or school boards require teacher certification for some of their classified positions, especially those that are academically related.
10. Number 10 is **false.** A job family is those job titles under one particular work area, such as food services, clerical/secretarial, custodial/maintenance, instructional aide and assistance or health/safety. A job family in a large school district might have as many as fifteen or more job titles within its classification.

If you answered seven or more of the questions on the pre-quiz correctly, you did well. Five to six correct answers gives you a light pat on the back. Less than five correct answers gives you an opportunity to gain more specific knowledge about classified personnel and the work of the school principal in contemporary schools.

The Classified Recruitment Process: Where It All Begins

Classified recruitment is more often administrated by the human resources director's office at the district level. However, the supervision of maintenance workers, administration of job orientation, completion of performance evaluations, implementation of employee-development programs and fostering of job-retention activities for classified personnel become cooperative responsibilities of the classified office personnel at the district level and the local school principal. Thus, the school principal generally serves as the immediate supervisor of classified employees serving in his or her school. We submit that the classified staff at the local level will increasingly be recognized as being of paramount importance to the accomplishment of the local school's goals and objectives.

> Classified school employees play a vital role in the education of our pupils and students in our public schools . . . They do essential work that keeps our campuses safe, clean, and well maintained so that our pupils and students can get to school, focus on learning, and succeed at their highest levels.
>
> (California Senate, 2013)

It is clear that the work performed by the classified employees at the local school is essential for accomplishing the stated mission of the school.

We submit that the school principal's personnel administration at the local school level will continue to change and increase in authority. That is, a school principal will become increasingly involved in all of the HR processes, and will remain as the leader of the human resources function in his or her school. However, we believe that the assistant school principal or a school operations manager will assume the responsibility for many of the HR processes that will continue to increase at the local school level. The hiring of such an employee most likely will not be possible for all sizes of schools, but schools with larger school populations will benefit by employing such an administrator. Figure 6.1 is an example of a job description for a school operations manager that supports the school principal by assuming many of the current position responsibilities of the school principal in the administration of general school operations, including the HR function.

Your first reaction to the addition of a position at the local school level, as illustrated in Figure 6.1, is likely that, "we can't afford to do it, budget-wise." Think of ways that you might convince yourself and others that you cannot afford not to do so.

Some Changes Require a Bold Stand

One school superintendent told the story about how he received the school board's approval to hire a purchasing agent. The schools had been expending rather large sums of money for film and other media rentals, purchasing individual appliances and instructional equipment throughout the school year, and purchasing certain audio-visual equipment that sat infrequently used in one classroom in a school. At a regular meeting of the school board, the superintendent set forth a challenge. He stated that if such a position was approved and a purchasing agent was hired, that he guaranteed that the monetary savings for the school district would be three times that of the new employee's salary over the first year and thereafter. The school board approved the new hire. After establishing a specific schedule for equipment orders from all personnel from all district schools and having all academic school leaders and teachers establish priority equipment lists for first priority, second priority and third priority materials, then ordering in quantities and obtaining purchasing bids, the challenge set forth by the school superintendent was not only reached, but savings far exceeded the new employee's annual salary.

Take a minute to think of a way that monetary savings might be possible if a school operations manager was employed in the school. For example, give thought to the cost of losing a classified employee and having to hire a replacement.

Position: School Operations Administrator

Position Purposes: Responsibilities center primarily on work related to the classified personnel function and to other non-academic duties related to organizational events and school facilities. The planning and implementation of the necessary classified processes of hiring, assigning, supervising and performance evaluating are performed under the supervision of the school principal.

Immediate Supervisor: The School Principal

Supervisory Authority: Supervises classified personnel assigned to the school.

Job Description

Specific Responsibilities:

Assumes a leadership responsibility in the recruitment and hiring of classified personnel at the school site under the policies and administrative regulations of the school and school district.

Supervises all classified personnel assigned to the school site.

Supports the school principal in the performance evaluation process for all classified employees according to the policies and administrative regulations of the school and school district.

Cooperates with the school principal and central human resources office of the school district in determining the professional growth and development needs of individuals and job families in the school and school district.

Serves as the source for reporting classified employee policy violations, including sexual harassment, substance abuse, work quality, insubordination and other problems related to the classified worker program.

Performs other non-academic duties, such as scheduling and management of school events in school facilities or on the school campus, improvement of school safety and security, school discipline or other related duties as delegated by the school principal.

Knowledge and Skill Requirements of the Position:

Is knowledgeable of the school district's policies and the administrative regulations pertaining to the position, including the federal and state laws relating to the rights of classified employees in hiring, assigning, orienting, evaluating and suspending/terminating classified personnel.

Has the ability to communicate effectively with others orally and in written communication.

Practices the appropriate interpersonal skills necessary for working with classified employees, school patrons, students and other members of the school-community.

Is knowledgeable of the best practices for administering the classified personnel program and has the skills to perform the required duties of the position.

FIGURE 6.1. Sample Job Description of the School Operations Administrator

Has a basic knowledge of budgeting and accounting practices as related to the reporting requirements of the position.

Understands and practices the principles of effective administration, supervision and leadership.

Specific Administrative Skills Necessary for Effective Job Performance:

Is able to plan effectively in relation to the human resources function for classified personnel.

Understands and practices the process of recruiting and hiring quality personnel, and is able to present evidence of accountable employee results.

Practices appropriate assignment practices that emphasize the utilization of the employee's personal interests and strengths.

Possesses the ability to implement viable formative and summative evaluation procedures for all job classifications in place at the school site.

Understands and practices the traits of cooperation, support and fairness in dealing with individuals in relation to the needs and problems of the school's classified employees.

Provides a wide range of growth and development activities for employees in tune with the employee's plan for personal improvement.

Maintains appropriate records of employment for all classified employees in accord with the requirements of federal, state and local laws and regulations.

Uses hard data activity results to illustrate the classified program's success, in terms of employee retention, quality production, growth and development, and other dimensions of personnel activity.

FIGURE 6.1. *continued*

> It is estimated that it cost 25% to 33⅓% of the teacher's salary to replace him or her . . . By using the 25% figure, lose only 10% of a staff of 130 teachers making an average salary of $36,000 and the bill is $117,000, money that would be welcomed in other budget lines.
>
> (Norton, 2008, p. 179)

We do not have research data that we can use for determining accurately the cost of losing classified personnel, but empirical evidence suggests that the attrition of classified personnel is much higher than for certificated employees; many classified personnel leave the school for higher salaries in the business and industrial fields. But for the purpose of illustration, let's use an example of a school that has 30 classified employees and it loses 50% of them after only the first year. Just the administrative costs of a new hire are estimated to be

$5,000. If the classified employee's average salary is $25,000 and the school loses 50% of its 30 classified employees, the bill is $75,000. If we estimated the salary of a new full-time school operations administrator as being $55,000 a year, we also could estimate some savings with the new employee. Losing a certified or classified employee is not only expensive monetarily, but the cost of orienting and developing those employees and then having to do it all over again with a new hire is costly as well. The operations manager's role could also be assigned to a new employee, to a new assistant principal, or to a present school employee who possesses the job qualifications.

The Principal's Responsibilities for Classified Personnel Are Commonly Determined by the Composition of the School District

In the following sections of this chapter, the human resources function is discussed as it applies to the local school administration. As a school principal, the composition of the school district in which you serve will predict the responsibilities that you have regarding the administration of the classified employees. For example, the school district's food services director might supervise all cafeteria workers. Or the cafeteria manager at the local school might be the cafeteria workers' supervisor. In other instances, the school principal serves as the supervisor of the school's cafeteria workers. The foregoing example serves to point out the wide variety of administrative arrangements for classified personnel, depending on the size of the school district, the support services provided and other factors relating to school location and budgetary provisions.

In any case, your knowledge relative to the HR processes that encompass the classified staff will serve you well in whatever role you find yourself in leading the administration of the HR function for classified personnel. Classified personnel, sometimes referred to as support staff, commonly could be expected to constitute 20 percent to 30 percent of a school district's employees. Think of that for a moment. At the local school, the principal can expect at least one-fifth, and perhaps almost one-third, of the school personnel to be in the classified personnel category.

The Primary Position Families of Classified Personnel

We define the term **classified personnel** as those employees who are in a school district position that does not require certification. This definition does not imply that such employees do not require special position qualifications or have not completed specific training in their areas of employment.

Depending largely on the size of the school district, classified employees generally fit in one of the following job families. At the school district level, the additional job family of business/accounting would be necessary. This job family includes such employee positions as buyer, accountant, payroll clerk, budget control clerk and others. The following job families and related work positions are generally found at the local school level.

- **Paraprofessional**—teacher aides, teacher assistants, library aides, pupil services aides, clerical or administrative support personnel, secretaries.
- **Maintenance/Custodial**—carpenter, custodian, appliance repair worker, electrician, groundskeeper, office machines repair, painter and others.
- **Office/Clerical**—attendance clerk, typist, operations secretary, staff secretary, textbook clerk, supplies clerk, receptionist and others.
- **Food Services**—food production worker, food service clerk, food service aide, food service cashier/accountant, school lunch worker and others.
- **Security/Safety**—truancy officer, security officer, grounds patrol worker, safety officer.

Job Analyses and Position Descriptions as Related to Classified Personnel

The topics of the job analysis and position description as they pertain to certificated personnel were discussed previously in Chapter 2. The need for position analyses and specific position descriptions for classified personnel is equally important. Although we will review the definitions of a job analysis and position description, our human resources focus in this chapter is on the classified personnel working at the local school level. Once again, it seems important to point out that the HR function in schools nationally is a cooperative administrative endeavor between the HR office of the school district and the school principal at the local school level. Not in all cases will you be responsible for administering certain activities of the classified HR function. Nevertheless, your knowledge and understanding of the classified HR function, its importance and complexity, will serve you well in working with classified staff members in your school and within the school district.

A **classified job analysis** is the process of examining the contents of a job and breaking it down into its significant tasks. It is a scientific, in-depth analysis

1. The Job Itself—duties, workload, tools needed, knowledge and skills required, growth requirements.
2. The Job Qualifications—abilities, physical requirements, necessary experience.
3. The Job Schedule—time requirements, tasks that influence the job, day/night work requirements, leave schedule, part-time/full-time.
4. Effects of the Job on the Worker—stress, turnover, relationships, sitting/standing/walking.
5. Relationship of the Job to the School and School District—coordination, supervision given, supervision received, reporting responsibilities.
6. Relationship of the Job to the School-Community—contacts, resources, support services, communication responsibilities.

FIGURE 6.2. Primary Contents of a Job Analysis for Classified Personnel

of a job, its constituent parts and surrounding conditions. Figure 6.2 includes the major contents of a classified job analysis.

A comprehensive, detailed form is commonly utilized to gather specific information for answering the entries listed in Figure 6.2 and for gaining in-depth information about the job from experienced workers and qualified supervisors. The actual form utilized by school districts and school leaders to gather the required information is far too lengthy to include in this chapter. However, an excerpt of a job analysis questionnaire is presented in Figure 6.3. In some instances, only the question being asked of the worker is presented in the figure, without the full details of the specifics and related information being required. A job analysis questionnaire is an information form that serves the purpose of finding specific information about a job from those individuals that are experienced in that job family and others that are serving in supervisory capacities related to that work.

By using the information provided by all workers in the same job, a more comprehensive and valid job description can be developed. Where do you obtain other data? In many instances, the school principal has ample opportunities to observe classified personnel on the job. Some school districts' central human resources offices and school principals have used employee diaries or job breakdown charts to record ongoing work activities. Supervisor analyses of work records and records of complaints, absences and exit interviews are other sources of job data.

Once again we ask the question, "Is all this work worth the trouble?" Of course, completion of a job analysis enables you to derive a more effective position description. In addition, a position analysis provides several significant benefits to you as principal, to the present position holder, and to future candidates for the position in question. Give a moment's thought to what you really know about the work of your cafeteria manager or head custodian. As principal, you do see them at work every day, but what about the answers that would most likely be given by the worker to questions IV, VII or XI in Figure 6.3? And how might the information gained be of special benefit to you as you administer the HR function in the school?

Snapshot 1—A Lightbulb Experience

Whittier Middle School had implemented a scientist-for-teacher day once a year, whereby local science-related individuals in the school community were asked to assume the role of a teacher while the science teachers took part in scheduled professional growth activities. The invited scientists did not follow lesson plans set forth by the regular classroom teacher; rather, they presented aspects of science and technology from the point of view of their business or industry. The visiting scientists did, however, meet with five different classes and serve as the "teacher" for the full day.

Paul Jensen, chief engineer of the local telephone company, was one of the visiting teachers for the scientist-for-teacher day at Whittier. He started his assignment at 8:30 a.m. and taught through the day until 3:30 p.m. At the end of the final sixth-period class, Paul found his way to the school office and met with the school principal, Emory Ross. Paul did look rather tired as he sat back in his chair.

"Well," asked Principal Ross, "How did it go, Paul?"

Paul didn't respond immediately, but took a deep breath and then replied, "Do teachers really do this every day?"

We often assume that we know what others do in their positions at work. After all, as a school principal, you see most of the faculty members and staff quite often. A job analysis has many benefits to both the school principal and the worker. One of the primary benefits of a job analysis for the principal is getting to know and understand the actual job requirements and the conditions and problems related to the work environments of the certificated faculty and classified staff members. One primary benefit for the employee is learning that the school principal is sincerely interested in knowing about the work conditions and requirements of the job at hand.

JOB ANALYSIS QUESTIONNAIRE

Directions: This is to request your help in furnishing information for the development of your job description and a job classification system for your job family. Please answer and/or describe as best you can the characteristics and factors of your job and the job qualifications as requested in each of the following entries.

I. In this section, the employee's name and location, immediate supervisor, and other contact information is detailed.

II. JOB DESCRIPTION: In this section, the position title, length of work year, present salary, official position title, full-time/part-time, and a listing of the *most important tasks of the position* are to be listed.

III. What are the additional tasks and responsibilities of this job that must be performed?

IV. Describe the physical conditions under which you work and any unusual situations: such as interruptions, noise, confusion, disturbances, etc.

V. Is it necessary for you to handle sums of money as a responsibility of this job? Please explain.

VI. How many people do you supervise, if any? Please list them, but exclude students.

VII. Identify the skills and knowledge that are necessary for serving satisfactorily in this position (e.g., typing certain number of words per minute, ability to repair school appliances, ability to read blueprints, ability to prepare a variety of foods for students, etc.).

VIII. List the types of equipment that you must be able to operate in your job. Please be specific and all-inclusive in your listing.

IX. Please identify the contacts that you believe best represent the human relations contacts of your job. Explain as best you can the nature of the contacts/communications of major importance.

X. The nature of your work demands what type of activity: such as sitting, standing, walking, climbing, carrying, etc.?

XI. List four of your job's most important activities and the approximate percentage of time that you must spend with each one.

XII. To what extent are you responsible for your own work? That is, do you determine primarily what you are to do; or is part of what you do assigned by another person; or is your work primarily given to you by another person?

XIII. What license or certificate is required for you to hold? In your opinion, what grade level is required to perform the tasks required of your job?

XIV. List your personal information concerning what growth and development requirements you have been required to meet to hold the position. List the licenses and certificates that you do hold.

FIGURE 6.3. A Job Analysis Questionnaire—An Excerpt

XV. List the present grade of your job. In your opinion, is this grade classification for your position a correct one?

XVI. Please list your educational history (grade completion, college work, business/vocational schools, other).

XVII. List the previous work experiences that you have had and give the approximate dates for this experience.

XVIII. List the kinds of supervision that you might provide in your present position. In addition, give some indication of the nature of this supervisory responsibility (e.g., work assignments, performance evaluations, orientation of new workers, service as a mentor or coach, etc.).

Your signature ____________________ Date ________________

FIGURE 6.3. *continued*

Most everyone in education knows about the early work of Elton Mayo (1933) and the Hawthorne effect. Mayo's studies at the Hawthorne plant at the Western Electric Company near Chicago found that what goes on inside the worker is more important in motivating workers than the physical conditions of the workplace. The attention given to the workers, their aspirations, and their interpersonal relationships and communication were the most important factors for fostering worker satisfaction, morale and work production.

A **classified job description** is derived from a comprehensive job analysis. Have you ever examined the job description of a school bus driver, a school cafeteria food service worker or a school custodian? If not, you most likely would be surprised at the job requirements. Figure 6.4 is an example of a custodian job description in a California unified school district. Since a position description has not been included in any of the earlier chapters of the book, a complete job description for one classified family job of custodian is presented.

The Classified Personnel Recruitment and Selection Processes

For all of the many school principals that were interviewed over a two-year time period, only one instance was found where the recruiting of classified candidates was led by the local school principal. The common practice is for the school district human resources office or the director of classified personnel in the school district to advertise for classified personnel, collect application

Class Title: Custodian
Class Code: 2013
Salary: Schedule

Description

Basic Function:
Under the direction of an assigned supervisor, perform routine day or evening custodial activities at an assigned school site; maintain buildings and adjacent grounds areas in a clean, orderly and secure condition.

Minimum Qualifications: Education and Experience
Any combination equivalent to: sufficient training and experience to demonstrate the knowledge and abilities listed above.

Licenses and Other Requirements
Some incumbents in this classification may be required to possess a valid state driver's license.

Representative Duties, Knowledge and Abilities
Perform routine custodial duties at an assigned district school site during a day or evening shift; sweep, scrub, mop, wax and polish floors; vacuum rugs and carpets in classrooms, offices, workshops and other work areas; spot clean and shampoo carpets.

Clean classrooms, cafeterias, lounges, offices and other facilities as assigned; dust and polish furniture and woodwork; empty waste receptacles; spot mop spills; remove gum, debris and graffiti as needed. Clean and disinfect drinking fountains and restroom facilities including sinks, toilets and urinals; fill dispensers with towels, soap, toilet paper and other items; clean mirrors, tile and windows; unclog drains and toilets. Pick up paper and other debris from school grounds, walkways and areas adjacent to school facilities; sweep concrete surfaces adjacent to the school building.

Replace light bulbs and tubes, clean chalkboards and erasers and empty pencil sharpeners; clean tables, chairs and floors after breakfast, lunch and recess periods as assigned. Lock and unlock doors and gates as appropriate; maintain security of assigned areas according to established guidelines; set alarms as appropriate.

Perform a variety of routine general maintenance and repair to equipment and furniture as assigned.

Report safety, sanitary and fire hazards to appropriate authority; report need for maintenance repairs to appropriate authority; respond to emergency custodial requests as needed.

Operate custodial equipment such as vacuums, mops, small hand and power tools, buffer/scrubber machines and other equipment as assigned. Move and arrange furniture and equipment; prepare classrooms and multipurpose rooms for special events or meetings; set up and assemble chairs, tables and other furniture and equipment for special events and activities; clean up furniture, equipment and debris following these events. Participate in the thorough cleaning and restoration of campus facilities during vacation periods.

Perform minor grounds management duties as assigned. Perform related duties as assigned.

FIGURE 6.4. Example of a Classified Job Description—Class Title: Custodian

Knowledge and Abilities: Knowledge of:

Proper methods, techniques, materials, tools and equipment used in modern custodial work.
Modern cleaning methods including basic methods of cleaning floors, blackboards, carpets, furniture, walls and fixtures.
Proper methods of storing equipment, materials and supplies.
Requirements of maintaining district building in a safe, clean and orderly condition.
Appropriate safety precautions and procedures.
Proper lifting techniques.

Ability to:

Perform routine custodial activities at an assigned school site.
Maintain district buildings and adjacent grounds in a clean, orderly and secure condition.
Use cleaning materials and equipment in a safe and efficient manner.
Operate a variety of custodial equipment.
Maintain tools and equipment in clean working order.
Move and arrange furniture and equipment for meetings and special events.
Observe and report hazards and needs for maintenance and repair.
Perform minor and non-technical repairs.
Understand and carry out oral and written directions.
Observe health and safety regulations.
Meet schedules and time lines.

Working Conditions: Environment

Indoor and outdoor work environment.
Regular exposure to fumes, dust and odors.
Driving a vehicle to conduct work as required by position.

Physical Demands:

Dexterity of hands and fingers to operate a variety of custodial equipment.
Walking or standing for extended periods of time.
Seeing to perform custodial duties.
Carrying, lifting, pushing or pulling moderately heavy objects.
Bending at the waist, kneeling or crouching.
Reaching overhead, above the shoulders and horizontally.
Climbing ladders and working from heights to replace light bulbs.

Hazards:
Exposure to cleaning agents and chemicals.
Working on ladders.

FIGURE 6.4. *continued*

form information, and evaluate such applications for possible work positions in the school district. In most cases, the central offices rated applications according to some appraisal system and conducted preliminary interviews of the applicants, often by telephone; then placed the most promising individuals in the candidate pool. The files of the best candidates were placed in a recruitment pool that was readily available to the school principals. So, all that the school principal had to do at that point is to post the specific classified position opening and select the candidate that he or she wanted to interview at the school.

The follow-up procedures for selection of employees from the candidate pool are illustrated in the following selection model. It is clear that the selection of classified personnel follows a model much the same as the model for selecting certificated personnel. There are differences, of course, but the processes virtually follow the same procedures.

The Selection of Classified Personnel: An Operational Model

1. The selection process for classified personnel should be determined by the selection policies of the school board and the administrative regulations determined by the school superintendent and administrative staff. Without a specific policy and/or regulation to follow, selection is likely to become spasmodic and lack the consistency of quality needed on the part of classified personnel.
2. By utilizing the list of qualified candidates that have been identified through the screening processes of gathering application data, interviewing strategies, background checks and reference information, the school principal selects those candidates that meet the job requirements in question according to the job description. Plans are made for selecting from the recruiting pool and conducting initial selection interviews.
3. An effective selection process requires an objective method of ranking classified candidates who have met minimal job requirements. Those candidates that have been appraised as having the highest qualification scores are reviewed once again to determine those with the highest qualifications for the job at hand.
4. Those candidates with the highest qualifications are then approved for additional testing by use of performance tests, simulation exercises, written examinations or other appropriate information procedures that lead to final selections.[1]

5. After all the data have been collected and assessed, a system consensus is implemented and eligibility lists are prepared.
6. Employee eligibility lists are prepared, and nominations of candidates for hiring are prepared. In some cases, recommendations of classified nominees for hire are presented to the school superintendent and then to the school board. In other cases, only the school superintendent's approval is required, or the approval is delegated to an assistant superintendent or to the director of human resources for the school district.
7. Following approval, the school principal or designated central office administrator sends appointment letters to successful candidates. Letters congratulate the new hires, but point out that the official hire is contingent on the school board's final approval and the completion of certain actions, such as the results of background checks.

Assessing the Classified Employee Selection Process

Some turnover of classified members is expected to take place. But one way to check the effectiveness of your selection, orientation and development processes is to examine the percentage of employees that were hired and assigned to your school and still remain after one, two and three years of service. Perhaps some of these workers advanced to higher-grade jobs within the school system, so these individuals need not be included in the count. But if you hired 15 different classified employees during the three-year time period and fewer than 50 percent of them are still with you, you'll need to examine these results. Some of them most likely left the school system for a higher paying job in the business sector; this perhaps can be expected. Minimally, you would need to consider the implementation of exit interviews, either in person or in written form.

An **exit interview** serves the primary purpose of determining the reason(s) that an employee is leaving a job in your school voluntarily. Is the reason tied to some unsatisfactory job condition within the school? Is the reason related to personal relationships or to factors connected with the job conditions? There is even a chance that the individual might decide to remain with you. However, even if this is not the case, perhaps you will identify a problem area that needs your attention. The information on teacher retention presented earlier in the book applies just as well to classified personnel. Personnel retention and re-recruitment strategies discussed in chapter 2 need to be administered for classified personnel as well. Once the classified candidate is hired, you need to implement plans to keep them. One strategy that you might consider is to set an accountability goal for classified personnel retention for the next three years. Plan the strategy for achieving your goal just as you would do with an academic achievement goal or certificated employee growth and development objective. Then implement your plan, and be prepared to pat yourself on the back in regard to the success that you certainly will realize.

We have found that school principals are the primary performance appraisers of classified personnel in their schools. The foregoing information will be most helpful to you for increasing your knowledge and skill in working with support staff members. However, classified employees have identifiable differences in the way in which they are classified, promoted and remunerated. The following sections discuss each of these factors.

Job Families and Job Grading Relative to Classified Personnel

Previously we introduced the topic of job families for classified personnel. Within a job family, there could be ten or more job titles with varying grade levels or pay scales for salary range purposes. For example, in the job family of clerical/secretarial, the job titles of clerk typist 1, clerk typist 2, attendance clerk, staff secretary, staff secretary bilingual, operations secretary and others are included. The completion of job analyses for each of these job titles provides information that is used to grade each job. Job grades are simply numbers that are used comparatively for similar positions within the job family and/or for comparison among job families. A job grade rating of 1 to 7, for example, would likely be appropriate for classified employees within a local school setting. For the school district, however, a grade rating would have to include many more pay scales in order to cover the many different classified titles. Pay scale listings differ from school district to school district, but typically include job titles and pay scales from low to high as follows: Pay Scale 1—intern or student worker; Pay Scale 2—custodian, food service worker, clerk typist, parent aide; Pay Scale 3—maintenance worker 1, food service manager, security guard, food service courier; Pay Scale 4—account clerk 1, typist clerk 2, attendance clerk, bilingual paraprofessional; Pay Scale 5—accounts payable clerk, administrative assistant, head custodian, buyer, library resource secretary, staff secretary, maintenance 2, secretary administrative services; Pay Scale 6—electrician assistant, senior buyer, operations secretary; and Pay Scale 7—school operations manager, electronics repair worker, accounting technician, journeyman plumber, carpenter.

Salaries for job titles are determined by a schedule similar to a certificated single salary schedule. Commonly, the salary schedule includes a column of ranges (grade ranges), years of experience, and hourly wages for each grade range and years of experience. Of course, salaries for classified employees at local school sites are equivalent to those working out of the district office. A journey plumber assigned to a local school and one working out of the central district office with the same years of experience would earn equivalent salaries if their work schedule were the same.

The Growth and Development Requirements for Classified Personnel: This Might Surprise You

You might be surprised to learn that the staff growth and development requirements for classified personnel commonly meet and even surpass such requirements for certificated personnel. In the case of classified personnel, in many school districts, growth and development requirements serve as the basis for employee salary increases and job retention. Among the surprises, perhaps, are the kinds of development classes and workshops that are provided for classified personnel in the nation's schools. Technical knowledge and skill improvement are important, but such topics as oral and written communication, interpersonal relationships, listening skills, teambuilding, conflict management, and valuing diversity are among the elective and required staff development topics of classified personnel offered by many school districts.

School principals are involved in the training opportunities for classified staff members in many ways. Mentoring and coaching relationships are among the development activities offered within the school by the school principal, assistant principal, school operations administrator, the head of classified personnel at the school site or the classified personnel director at the district office level. Training programs commonly are conducted with job family employees across the school district. The primary purposes of classified training programs are to update employees with the latest technology in their work assignment, and to assist them to achieve their maximum performance potential.

In most cases, staff development programs for classified employees include both elective and required training courses. Entry courses commonly consist of basic classes such as communication skills, conflict management, work safety, and teambuilding strategies. Elective courses in many development programs include workshops and/or classes in oral and written communication, workplace courtesy, time management, diversity in the workplace and healthful living. In the classified staff system, promotion and salary increases often are based on the employee's growth and development activities and their results in terms of job performance. Advanced classes for this purpose depend on the job family knowledge and skill requirements, but tend to focus on leadership and technical skills related to the job. For example, teambuilding, planning and organization, leadership styles, adult learning styles, supervision, training skills, and career development represent the kinds of classes found in most advanced classified workshops and training classes.

The central district office of human resources or classified personnel in many school districts cooperates with the local school principals in the offering of mentoring programs, internship programs and career management services. Tuition reimbursement programs, up to a certain monetary limit, also are available in most cases for employees to complete course work that is directly related to their jobs. The school principal must be knowledgeable of the various improvement opportunities for classified personnel, as he or she serves as a mentor or coach for this group of employees. In the large majority of instances, it is the school principal that serves as the supervisor and work performance evaluator of classified personnel that work at the school site. It is imperative that the school principal possesses the competencies necessary to help plan and implement the improvement activities for respective employees.

Tasks, Competencies and Indicators of Competencies Essential to the HR Function

The position description of high school principals in the New Haven Unified School District in Connecticut lists twenty-two essential functions of this administrative role. Five of these functions center directly on responsibilities relative to the school's classified personnel. In the New Haven Unified School District, the school principal:

1. Interviews, selects, directs, and evaluates certificated and classified personnel;
2. Coordinates the maintenance and operations of the school plant; assures proper management, maintenance and inventory of materials, equipment, buildings and grounds;
3. Directs the implementation of staff development and in-service training;
4. Plans and directs the business operations of the school; develops and administers site budgets; assures proper allocation of funds for instructional and non-instructional equipment and materials; and

Task	Competencies
1.0 To provide orientation, evaluation, and staff development of classified personnel assigned at the school site.	1.1 Demonstrates knowledge and understanding of the HR processes for classified personnel. 1.2 Ability to determine the needs of personnel growth and improvement as related to the employee's personal needs and job title. 1.3 Demonstrates knowledge and understanding of the concepts of human motivation and utilizes this ability to gain optimal employee performance and job satisfaction. 1.4 Ability to facilitate personnel development by providing opportunities for personal and professional growth.
2.0 To provide for supervision and evaluation of classified personnel.	2.1 Ability to organize and administer an effective program of supervision and performance evaluation of classified personnel according to state and local policies and regulations. 2.2 Ability to demonstrate knowledge of the legal aspects of employment of classified personnel including the negotiated agreements as fits the case. 2.3 Ability to cooperate with other offices and individuals in the school district in the administration of the classified HR processes.
3.0 To provide a school climate conducive to the discussion of human resources issues, problems and recommendations.	3.1 Ability to maintain a climate of openness and support through involvement of classified employees, including the personal interests and career goals of individuals. 3.2 Demonstrates the ability to assess the working environment of classified employees at the school by observation,personal communication and climate surveys.
4.0 To assist in the development of a system of compensation and benefits for classified personnel.	4.1 Ability to participate in the development of job descriptions and implementation of growth requirements as related to the compensation requirements for each job title, job promotion, and career development. 4.2 Ability to cooperate actively in the implementation of the payroll system for the school district in relation to contractual agreements, overtime pay, and merit salary increases as fits the case.
5.0 To establish a personal plan for his or her commitment to a program of professional development relative to the classified human resources function.	5.1 Ability to make a critical self-assessment of areas of needed growth relative to the human resources function, and establishing a program of personal improvement for working with classified personnel at the school site.

FIGURE 6.5. Tasks and Competencies Related to the Administration of the Classified Staff at the Local School Level

5. Directs the maintenance of comprehensive files pertaining to school personnel, plant facilities, inventories, financial information, and contracts; directs the maintenance of student and staff records on site (New Haven Unified School District, 2013).

Figure 6.5 centers on the tasks and competencies required on the part of the school principal for administering the classified human resources processes. As previously noted, depending on the school district and school's status, many of the tasks included in the listing are cooperatively planned, implemented and supervised by other individuals and offices within the school district. Nevertheless, the HR classified staff responsibilities increasingly are being delegated to the local school sites.

Summary

Chapter 6 emphasized the growing importance of the classified personnel function at the local school site, and the increasing responsibilities of the school principal for administering that function. The administration of classified personnel processes remains a cooperative endeavor between the local school principals and the human resources office at the school district level.

The classified staff membership has realized continuous growth over the last four decades. Many of the needed school services that previously were outsourced have been withdrawn and taken over by the local school district. The local school with its few custodians and secretaries now includes classified employees from numerous job areas. Such developments as extended student lunch provisions, safety and security measures, more and larger schools with more and larger repair needs along with related program aides and assistants have created new employees and employee needs at local school sites. These trends have demanded new knowledge and skills on the part of the school principal for the administration of the classified personnel function.

It is well known that the school principal's work responsibilities have increased greatly over the years. Academic mandates alone have increased the principal's workload. The need for additional administrative assistance at the local school level is evident, yet many schools, especially at the elementary school level, have yet to have an assistant principal on the administrative staff. Several options for adding additional service to the local school for administering the human resources function were discussed. Ultimately, we visualize a special operations manager to supervise the human resources function at the school level. The goal of attracting and retaining quality faculty and support staff demands such leadership.

The classified personnel program has both similarities and differences when compared to the certificated employees program. The organization of job families is evidenced in the classified employee program. In addition, each job family includes a variety of job titles that are described, analyzed and ultimately graded for purposes of compensation and promotion. It is common that salary schedules for classified personnel include years of service, job grade level, and commensurate hourly pay. As done with the single salary schedule of certificated personnel, with each year of service and promotions in grade ranges, classified employees receive additional hourly payments.

The development of job descriptions for classified employees is just as important as these tools are for certificated employees. Performance evaluations and related development plans tie closely to the requirements of the job description. In addition, the cooperative development of a classified employee's job description benefits both the employee and the school principal. A clearer understanding of a job's requirements by both parties lends to a better understanding of the job's purposes and suggests guidelines for identifying needed growth and development.

The selection of classified personnel follows a pattern similar to that of certificated personnel. For each of the HR processes of recruitment, selection, orientation, assignment and performance evaluation, a planned procedure is of paramount importance. Each process in most school districts is a cooperative activity that includes the school principal, other employees within the school and those individuals within the district office of human resources.

Common tasks and competencies of the classified human resources function required of school principals served to close the chapter. Empirical evidence indicates that preparation programs for school principals relative to human resources administration are minimal at best. Each practicing principal is encouraged to initiate a planned development program in the area of human resources administration; the payoff will be far-reaching.

Discussion Questions

1. The need for specific administrative service support at the local school level was emphasized throughout Chapter 6. Consider the reality of this recommendation. How, in your opinion, can such services be enhanced

at the local school level? Test in your mind the recommendations that were presented in the chapter relative to added services. Could any of the recommendations be implemented in your school or in a school with which you are most familiar? Why or why not?

2. What is meant by the term, job grading, as it applies to classified personnel? Explain the procedures for determining the job range ratings for several job titles within a specific job family.
3. As school principal, list several of the primary position challenges that you face in the administration of the human resources function. For each entry that you list, answer the three following questions: (a) How well were you prepared to administer each major HR challenge that you face? (b) In your opinion, how well are you handling the entries listed? and (c) Could any of the entries on your list be delegated to other members of your faculty under your supervision? If you are in the stage of preparing to become a school principal, answer the question in terms of your current opinions about the challenges to be faced.

Case Studies

Case 6.1. The Case of "That's Not My Job!"

Jim Heston was serving in his first year as custodian at Wymore Elementary School. He was selected by the school principal, Pat Garcia, from the district recruitment pool as one of the five most promising candidates. Except for several absences from work, Jim was seen as doing a satisfactory job as school custodian. He had participated in the principal's orientation sessions that centered primarily on the school's mission and the importance of the classified staff in meeting the academic goals of the school.

Jim worked beside two other school custodians, one of whom was assigned primarily to groundskeeping work. Elsie Miller was the other custodian that worked inside the school. After six weeks into the first semester, Principal Garcia began to receive comments from both students and faculty personnel that the school's restrooms were not being cleaned as needed. Sinks were clogged in two of the restrooms, and some students were avoiding the use of the restrooms due to the conditions of the floors and bad odors that prevailed.

It didn't take Principal Garcia long to confirm the condition of the restrooms, and she sent memos to each of the two "in-school" custodians to meet with her the next day after school.

As the three persons met in the principal's office, the principal opened by stating, "We have a real problem in our restrooms that needs immediate attention. I expect this situation to be taken care of immediately."

Jim Heston asked, "Which restrooms are they? I don't think mine are out of order in any way."

Principal Garcia replied, "One is the south girls' restroom on the first floor and the other is the south girls' restroom on the second floor."

"Neither one of these is mine," said Jim Heston.

Then custodian Elsie Miller interjected, "Well they're not mine either. Why are they mine and not yours?" she asked Heston. "I seem to be the restroom custodian in this place."

"Well," responded Heston, "Just because you are a . . ."

"Hold on Jim," demanded Principal Garcia, "I am trying to solve a problem, not create one!"

Question:

Re-read the case study again to be certain that you have caught all of the happenings and statements of this matter. Now, assume the role of Principal Garcia and set forth your immediate administrative actions/decisions at this point and time. You have to act now to take care of the matter at hand in your office. Set forth the specifics of your actions/statements to close the ongoing meeting. Then, take a step back and identify the restroom problem, and why and how this matter likely occurred. What human resources activities/steps might have been taken to obviate the current problem? As school principal, what HR actions are needed at this point in time?

Case 6.2. No Need for Negotiations This Year, We'll Just Take the Same Percentage Increase That the Teachers Get!

Paul Biggerstaff was serving as the chief negotiator for the classified employees of the Wymore School District. In the past, the classified personnel negotiations team always negotiated salary and conditions of work with the school district's negotiations team that consisted of two school principals, the school district's director of human resources and the assistant superintendent in charge of business. Due to rather difficult economic times, for the last two years classified personnel had not received salary increases; they did receive the experience increment provided by the next step on the salary schedule.

Kathryn Scott, Paul's school principal, was named to serve on the school district's negotiations team for a two-year term.

On one occasion, Paul and Principal Scott met in the school hallway.

Principal Scott smiled at Paul and said, "Hi Paul, all geared up for our negotiations this year?"

"Not really," responded Paul, "Our classified employees' association has made the decision to agree to the same salary percentage increase that the teachers get next year. I guess that we really don't plan to negotiate this year."

Principal Scott's smile faded. She could tell that Paul was not kidding about the matter. Not knowing exactly how to reply, she just smiled and said, "Well, see you later."

Question:

Have you ever given thought to the matter of salary discussions for the different employee groups that exist in your school district? Along with the certificated and classified personnel, teaching personnel in the areas of vocational/technical programs also exist. In some situations, health/nursing and library/media employees are not considered as certificated personnel. Most of the personnel in vocational/technical programs do not hold professional degrees, but do have course credits in their field and certifications in their areas of expertise. As a class activity or individually, discuss the personnel issues relative to compensation that could be encountered when working with two or more employee groups in the same school and school district. Include positive outcomes of such employee relationships, but also consider the potential outcomes of competition, social relationships, mission/goals, and other factors that a school principal is likely to encounter.

Notes

1. In an administrator academy in Arizona, this model was being discussed. In the discussion at point 4, one principal raised his hand and commented, "Getting classified personnel for our school is far more difficult. I just ask, "Are you breathing and able to come to work every day? If so, you're hired!"

References

California Senate. (2013, October 10). Senate Bill No. 590 (SB-590), School Personnel: Professional Development for Classified School Employees. Retrieved from http://leginfo.legislature.ca.gov/faces/billNavClient.xhtml?bill_id=201320140SB590

Mayo, E. (1933). *The human problems of an industrial civilization.* New York, NY: Macmillan.

New Haven Unified School District. (2013, December 12). *High school principal.* New Haven, CT: New Haven Unified School District.

Norton, M. S. (2008). *Human resources administration for educational leaders.* Thousand Oaks, CA: Sage.

Index

Note: 'f' indicates a figure.